ANCHOR
BOOKS

INSPIRING THOUGHTS

Edited by

Sarah Andrew

First published in Great Britain in 2002 by
ANCHOR BOOKS
Remus House,
Coltsfoot Drive,
Peterborough, PE2 9JX
Telephone (01733) 898102

HB ISBN 1 84418 006 9
SB ISBN 1 84418 007 7

FOREWORD

Anchor Books is a small press, established in 1992, with the aim of promoting readable poetry to as wide an audience as possible.

We hope to establish an outlet for writers of poetry who may have struggled to see their work in print.

The poems presented here have been selected from many entries. Editing proved to be a difficult task and as the Editor, the final selection was mine.

I trust this selection will delight and please the authors and all those who enjoy reading poetry.

Sarah Andrew
Editor

Sisters
  On page 138

Written by:-
    Susan Carol Roberts

CONTENTS

TALES OF AN OLD SALT

Home is the sailor, home from the sea, aware that this trip is his last.
He fingers a gold brooch of fine filigree with memories born of his past.
Two names in a wild rambling rose are entwined and the sun brings its
beauty to life.
He doesn't need brooches to bring to his mind the rose whom he took
for his wife.
The years spent while he mastered the waves will from now on not keep
them apart.
He's seen many comrades meet watery graves and is thanking the Lord
from his heart,
That his faithful craft 'Seabird' had come home to rest with his crew all
safely aboard.
He's spent his life putting his strength to the test and this homecoming
is his reward.
He has children and grandchildren waiting to hear the yarns he has kept
in his head.
He'll tell them the tales with the sea ever near and hear sounds of the
sea from his bed!
For a sailor can never be bound to the land, the call of the ocean
is strong.
He would see it and smell it out there on the strand and he prayed that
his life would be long.
Approaching the harbour, he struck a proud pose for the folk who were
waiting to cheer,
And in front of them all stood his treasure, his Rose who, most of all in
the world he held near.

Eileen Martin

LAST REQUEST

Please plant a rosebush on my grave
My love, and do not grieve, be brave.
I do not crave a marble stone.
A stone is cold and leaves me all alone.

A rosebush full of summer flowers
Exuding scent in rainy showers.
How like my life in sun and rain
Brimful of gladness and of pain.

Yes! Full of sadness and despair
And yet, what joys so deep and rare.
Your love and laughter, what delight
And friends to make my whole life bright.

Your hand in mine - love does not die
It forms an everlasting tie
From you to me, from man to wife
It does not even end with life.

Please plant a rosebush, not a stone
That I may never feel alone
Where birds may nest and gaily sing
Of courtship and eternal spring.

Gertrude Black

THE SLAVE'S RETURN

Beside ripened sugar cane,
He lay without a sound.
This body that was noble,
Dying on the ground.
Then in the midst of his mortal sleep,
An African breeze softly blew.
He beheld a wondrous vision,
And saw the land he knew.

This vision of his homeland,
Made him rejoice that he was free.
It echoed his liberation,
From a long captivity.
The kraal walls were stout and strong.
He heard the native cry.
Tears of joy came over him,
As a flock of birds flew by.

Lions were basking in the sun.
Flamingos arose from a lake.
A cheetah began to swiftly run;
As the earth from sun did bake.
Jackals, hyena and zebra.
African dogs on a spree.
Springboks dancing in the air;
On African plains so free.
Diverse, natural beauty.
Creation's wondrous song.
He was in joyful harmony,
And at last with God belong.

Denis A Walsh

FLAMING JUNE

(Inspired by the painting of the same name by Frederick Lord Leighton)

Reclining in her window bay,
Flaming June, asleep she lay.
Dreaming of a horseman riding,
Secrets she is not confiding.

Only she can see his face,
In his eyes she hopes to gaze.
Charging forward, his armour shining,
Helmet hiding his face, beguiling.

Forever hoping her dreams come true,
Sadly lovers passing by are few.
As years pass by her desires waver not,
For she's the one who love forgot.

Susan Martin

THE FROG AND THE PRINCESS

A frog and a princess met while walking out one day,
'Hello my lovely princess, won't you stop and play?'
'I never play with frogs,' said she 'they are slimy, wet and cold,
And how dare you speak to me, you really are too bold.'
'But if you will give me a kiss, I'll turn into a prince.'
'Don't ask me that's impossible,' the princess told the frog
'You really are too much for me go jump into the bog.'
'Oh princess don't forsake me, I've loved you from afar.'
'If you don't be quiet frog, I'll shut you in a jar.'
But the frog persisted and she then gave him a kiss
He stood there beautiful, hair of gold and clothes of purest silk.
His frog days were over and he gave her a wink
'Aren't you glad you kissed me?' he said with a smile.
She gazed at him with loving eyes, and then she thought a while,
If I hadn't gone a walk today, and met the frog upon the way,
I would go home all alone, to a palace made of stone,
But now I've met my lovely prince, I'll never walk alone.

Dorothy Brown

BON VOYAGER

I've sailed the mighty oceans
Roved the seven seas
Hit a typhoon in the Bengal Bay
A hurricane's fearsome breeze

The placid South Pacific
Where flying fishes play
The dolphin and the marlin
Follow us all day

I've sailed the roaring Forties
Where you could hardly stand
The heaving lips and downs
Without a sight of land

I've crossed the line with Neptune
Gained another day
In the great Pacific Ocean
Where the trade winds play

The Panama and Suez canals
Modern wonders to enfold
The great ships that took me
On voyages to behold.

Derriek Harding

THE GERIATRIC WARD

Is your mother here, and does she sit and cry?
Knowing she is somewhere strange, but not really knowing why?
She had a home, a husband and family,
Now she seems to have lost her identity;
Does her wandering mind recall
Any of her past at all?

Is your grandmother here, and does she know
What led to her coming here, some time ago?
She had a life, like you and I,
She'll suddenly remember, and she'll cry.

We may look at them all, and think with a sigh
That there, but for the grace of God, go you, and you - and I.

Georgia B Jones

LAMENT

Now wouldn't you say, that a French beret,
Led a truly tranquil life,
If I were one I'd get ahead,
But I needn't get a wife.

On the other hand, as a silk hatband,
I could travel near and far,
One day I'd be on an Alpine rim,
Then off to Panama.

While gabardine maces and corduroy slacks
Have my unrequited love,
They're not as tame, though they're much the same
As the shoe bag and the glove.

But I couldn't be an anorak,
No matter what the fee,
For watching birds and spotting trains,
Just ain't my cup of tea.

Oh if only I were an old school tie,
I'd go straight to the top,
But alas I am resigned,
To being just . . . a sock.

Colin Hart

MOWER MANIA

My husband has a mania for mowing all the lawn,
He's out there mowing merrily as soon as it is dawn,
I expect you think, well after all that's really not too bad,
But you haven't heard the worst of it, it's really rather sad.

He'll buy a brand new mower, then out he'll go to mow,
Humming along quite happily, cutting down each row,
I sit indoors and listen, waiting for the groan,
You see I know it's going to happen, silence! He's hit a stone.

'Don't worry,' he says every time, smiling sweet at me,
'I'll mend it, mend it?' Thinks I, this I've got to see,
Soon there's bolts and nuts and screws, piled up everywhere,
'I think I'll put it in the shed' says he, 'it must be wear and tear.'

And so into the shed it goes, in with all the others,
Oh yes there's lots of them looking all like brothers,
In fact there's rows and rows of them, lined up just like an army,
And if I go near that shed I'm sure they glare at me.

I had a dream the other night, they were marching side by side,
Getting ever closer I had nowhere to hide,
I tried to run, my legs were weak, I thought they were going to get me,
I woke up just in time, oh it did upset me.

I'm going to move into a flat, a flat with a window box,
He can't surely mow without a lawn, however much it shocks,
And if somebody buys this house, remember what I've said,
Whatever else you do, just don't go in the shed.

Sylvia Derbyshire

LIVING

Through the windows of my life
I see so much pain
Intertwined with all of this
Runs a bright refrain.
Pain and sorrow, happiness
Are blended all in one.
So how much more is available
With beauty yet to come
My troubles seem like stones
Along a lonely road
But joys are like an everlasting hill
Which outweighs all the load.

Eileen Burlingham

CONFRONTATION AT ARMAGEDDON

The Almighty who made Adam out of the dust of the ground
Could also have fashioned Eve of the identical compound;
Instead, He took one of Adam's ribs and made it a woman,
So to be his co-procreator, spouse, and companion!
Bidding them to be faithful, and fill the Earth, and multiply,
But not to be barren, immoral, or foetuses destroy.
The selfsame charges made He also to the animal world,
And they have adhered to it through the ages a hundred fold:
But man, overruling God, a great scandal has legalised,
And the sanctity of the unborn child, man has vilified.
Love, in consummation, creates an angelic Cherubim,
Lust, in its kinky sex game, also creates a Seraphim!
Whereas one is revered and treasured - an angel of delight,
Sadly, the other is aborted, and buried out of sight!
Three decades of abortion - forty-five million dead world-wide -
Have spilt enough life blood to fill a mighty ocean beside!
Shame to man that we, in this regard, are worse then animals,
Who exercise restraint - but not their abortive potentials:
Every aborted foetus had an inherent right to life,
Though an embryo, yet a human for God to recognise!
In the fullness of time, the abortion/Holocaust victims,
Among whom could have been myriads of Napoleons and Darwins,
Einsteins, Aristortles, Miltons, Gandhis, Hitlers and Flemmings,
Helens, Dianas, Teresas, Nightingales, Lincolns and Chopins,
Their Armada will invade, sailing the ocean of their blood,
And confront cruel exterminators in a tidal flood!
At Armageddon, they'll be indicted of first degree homicide,
And to inferno Hades, sans parole, for infanticide . . .

Welch Jeyaraj Balasingam

Two Broken Hearts

A long time ago, in the year '59,
Two young lovers they pledged, both to be thine.
The girl, she was Heather, the boy, he was Bill,
Young love was hard, as there was not, the pill.
The sea bade its calling, and they drifted apart,
Two young lovers, both, with a broken heart.
A child with no father, was loved as a son,
A daughter, borne, by the other one.
Time passed along, as the years rolled by,
Two wedding beds were made, and there, they must lie.
The young lovers they were, had now grown old,
A pledge they carried, would never be cold.
Two young lovers they met, the year '74,
The boy he was Bill, the girl, Eleanor.
Young love was to bloom - but should not be,
For half brother and sister, known only to thee.
The two older lovers, they met up by chance,
Their marriages crippled, as they looked for romance,
Tears at the table, as they all had their say,
Both joy and sadness, filled that day.
Two hearts had been broken - now there was . . . four.

William A B Mennie

THE QUALIFIER

Wednesday 17th November in 1993,
Saw England and San Marino scoring goals, one, two, three,
Group two was in a state of great disarray,
England needed seven to save the day.

The World Cup qualifier was turning into a great fight
Poland had to beat Holland, to give England some sight,
Wales playing Romania also needed to win,
However that easy penalty did not go in.

At the end of the night of complete dismay,
England and Wales didn't need to play,
Holland beat Poland with great Dutch might;
England beat San Marino but the target wasn't in sight.

So in 1994 England's not going to the US of A,
But keep smiling lads, there be another day,
Four years is not so long to hope and pray
As in '66 we'll bring the cup home - one day.

Dave Wright

LAUGHTER

Where does it hide, the laughter which we bring
Into this woeful world, at hour of birth?
Why do we let it go, this happy thing?
So much of joy departs, so little mirth
Remains, as babe grows into man, striving
To gather riches, making of this Earth
A something beyond price, or just nothing
But platform for success, for what it's worth.
Losing all sense of fun, the fun we bring
Into this woeful world at hour of birth.

Joan Head

PEACE IN OUR TIME

We have the joy of peace in Belfast
A fragile peace it may well be
Belfast for all your weary people
Peace has now become reality
Peace in our time has been my vision
And many share this dream of mine
Let us give thanks for the blessing
The blessing of peace in our time.

Belfast you have shared our sorrows
On your streets we shed our tears
We were afraid of our tomorrows
We lived every day with our fears
In the past it seems we lost our reason
Then we lost our common-sense
Then we had those scenes of carnage
That came from the mindless violence.

Belfast dear old weary Belfast
You've had your share of troubled times
And our future it is still uncertain
We have many mountains yet to climb
When we sit and talk around a table
We should think of the children yet to come
I hope that we can never go back to
Those days of the bomb and the gun.

Alex McConnell

FLAVOURED KISSES

How incredible it would be
If kisses could be flavoured
Simply fascinating to see
How many might be savoured.

Multi-flavoured profferings
Stretching through the day
These would improve life's offerings
More than one can say.

A peppermint kiss very first thing
Refreshing and clean at dawn
A flavour that will certainly cling
Serving to stifle a yawn.

An apricot kiss at eleven
Tart, yet sweet as can be
Could even be repeated at seven
Just in time for tea.

A strawberry kiss with a picnic lunch
Is a really splendid thought
An aperitif for a delightful munch
Perhaps a salmon freshly caught?

Mid-afternoon - a kiss of honey?
Light, not dark, like a winter's eve
Reminding one of days that are sunny
And another flavour to achieve.

A marmalade kiss is a matter of skill
To get the ingredients right
It could give a person a ferocious thrill
If planted by day or by night.

Dinnertime could be . . . 'any old flavour time'
Damson, lemon, raspberry or lime
Indeed any flavour at all that's fine
. . . and dandy.

At the end of a day that started so bright
Problem - what flavour with which to finish?
It's hard to choose such a taste at night
It could be anything from avocado to spinach!

Paul Harvey Jackson

ALL IN THE MIND

My young friend 'Lovejoy' must be nearly 70
To feel he is 'ageing' down below, never like 20
He needs a weekly tablet to restore the upturn glow
Never take too many or the thing may never go
Balance of judgement rising aloft falling soft
The trouble is he thinks about it daily more 'oft
Come night-time he is miles away
On flights of fancy with nothing to say
When little things need loving care
It's not enough just to be there
Then drop off unaware.

Take me for instance at 94
Many friends come knocking at the door
Maybe I am dreaming but couldn't ask for more
Gorgeous and beautiful things come all night long
Like popping into Heaven for ecstatics in song
Little things still working as of long ago
The mind rather than 'below' come again all aglow
With love at second sight, restoring all life's flow
Love's pleasures never ending, until we go.

Paff

THE BABY

After completing nine months
Growing increasingly fat
You produce a small baby
As easy as that

You've just had a baby
A bundle of joy
Now everyone's asking
Is it a girl or a boy?

But more questions will come
From all whom you meet
Your friends and your family
And those down the street

What weight is the baby?
Is everything well?
What name have you chosen?
There's so much to tell

As soon as you're home
The visitors start
They steadily come
And slowly depart

But things will calm down
As the well wishers go
It's just at the minute
Your baby's on show

You've just had a baby
Who'll look up to you
So be a good role model
In all that you do.

J L Preston

OLD AGE

What happens to our dreams when the years pass us by,
Where goes all those hopes, who's memories bring a sigh.
There must be a place where time can renew,
The things and the people who once we all knew.
But what happens to our dreams when we grow old?
When not so eager, not so bold.
Are they just fool's illusions? Ah! Who knows.
I'm just a daft old man, my, how time goes!

A G Teesdale

LEAVING HOME

I'm going to live with Aunt Helen and Harry,
My suitcase is packed, it's too heavy to carry.
Mummy and Daddy don't want me here,
It's my sister's fault, that much is clear.
She's been telling tales, whinging and whining,
Sniggering and simpering while they are dining.
Pushing and punching, when we are playing,
Mimicking every word that I'm saying,
She's been screaming and throwing herself on the floor,
Shouting and swearing and kicking the door.
When I'm watching TV she's hissing and booing,
She's trying to spoil everything that I'm doing.
My parents say, that she must behave,
Or else, they will be in an early grave,
They say it's my fault, how can it be?
They say my sister is copying me!
So, I'm going to live Aunt Helen and Harry,
My suitcase is packed, it's too heavy to carry.
I hate my sister, I hate everything about her,
And I'm not coming home 'til my parents shout at her.

C Karalius

MY BIRTHDAY

Today is my birthday
Another year on
A year full of sadness
For friends that have gone.
A year full of gladness
Especially for me
For now I'm bionic
In a part you can't see.
And as the times passes
And my family grows
Into young lads and lasses
Then my memory goes
Back to my childhood
When my life began
For today is the day
I remember my mam.

Mary Wise

THE CRUISE

I'd waited half a lifetime for that very special day
When I would pack my case and then sail away
To go to some exotic lands where I had never been
And just like in the brochure see sights I'd never seen

I went and booked the tickets and couldn't wait to go
The months though passing quickly to me seemed very slow
Then all at once the day was here my waiting at an end
To the coach I went with glee together with my *friend*.

We reached the ship and found our way to the cabins I had booked
These were as in the brochure exactly as they looked
I knew I would enjoy myself I'd waited for so long
It made me feel so happy, how could I be so *wrong*?

I don't want to see a show tonight, I don't really like the food
I'm not impressed at all by this, the stewards seem so rude
'Why do we have to go ashore? I want to go to bed'
I just could not believe this is what she'd said!

'You should come to shops with me, not let me go alone
Why don't you get my photos?' which made me give a groan
Oh how I wish I had not come, it wasn't what I thought
My nerves were in a tangle and I really felt quite fraught.

Could I stand ten days of this - I was getting in a state
I sat inside my cabin and cried at my sad fate
This nightmare nearly sent me completely round the bend
Next year I think what I should do is go down to *Southend*!

Letitia Snow

SHE DOES NOT SPEAK TO ME NOW

When John Gregory was born,
  He was more than meek and mild,
He could shout and do everything better
  Than any other child.
He cut his teeth much sooner
  Than my Nick ever did
And, oh, how his mother boasted
  About her clever kid!
When we met in the lane and stopped
  To have a little chat,
She would say, 'My John sits up by himself'
  When my Nick was still lying flat.
I got fed up with Mrs G,
  And said so at home loud and clear.
'I can't stand that woman!' I cried aloud
  Forgetting my three year old could hear.
So next time I stopped to chat
  When out on our usual walk
'You said you could not stand her' my daughter shrilled
  'So why do you stand and talk?'
The next time I saw Mrs Gregory
  My sickly smile was in vain
For she wheeled her precious child straight past
  And never spoke to me again.

Win Wilcock

ALWAYS REMEMBER

A time of joy,
a time of sorrow,
but don't look back,
look forward to tomorrow.

Treasure your memories
of those you hold dear.
The love that they gave
will keep them near.

Julie Brown

THOUGHTS OF FREELAND NOW

The rain falls like the tears of God
Tears of sorrow, of things I once had
I sit in the churchyard and think of the pain
Of the lives of all the people there lain
The village has changed so very much
Shop closed, post office and such
Children's happy voices as they race from school
When grown up they will leave, I'm no fool
Houses for sale, sadness fills the air
Why is it like this, doesn't anyone care?
The strong wind blows my hair trying to say
Nothing is the same as it was yesterday
I have so many memories of this special place
But all I can see takes the smile from my face
Traffic whizzes past at lightning speed
All that people want seems to speak of greed
I return to the convent where there is peace
Where I can escape, momentarily at least
The tulip tree still stands tall and serene
Seems to say it understands what's gone between
I miss the creaky chairs, clock that ticked too loud
The cast iron bath with legs that stuck out proud
Rooms with only lino, no heat to keep you warm
All this spoke of poverty but had a special charm
No dishwasher then, you used the kitchen sink
So many, many changes, really makes you think
Lighten up I tell myself, you can't live in the past
But what surrounds me now, I just can't grasp
One thing however, fills my heart with praise
My Saviour never changes, no matter how the days.

Veronica Quainton

FOOT AND MOUTH

In England's green and pleasant land
No spring has ever been so bleak.
On fell and dale a rural scene
Yet nowhere is the view we seek.

The gold of daffodil still bright
But silence proves the grief we feel.
No animals to gladden sight
Just circumstance a cause to kill.

No frolic of a new born lamb
No herd of cows to wander by.
This deadly virus has proclaimed
These animals will have to die.

The stench of smoke and funeral pyre
Obliterates the scent of flowers.
Farmer villager alike will fret
Away the lonely hours.

For all will pray they will regain
The sights and sounds they want to hear.
To walk again a country lane
Normality with no more fear.

Molly Phasey

JUNGLE

Deep in the jungle what gave us such a surprise
Was the natural wildlife that met our eyes
The colours and patterns everywhere
Of creatures that crawled or flew in the air
Our calm old elephant lumbered along
Well fed on bananas kept them fit and strong
Tired and exhausted we reached our destination
A wooden shack on stilts with no communication
The warm welcome we received served us so well
We did not care it was not a first class hotel
A smiling host served up a good meal
Which was rice, noodles, insects and orange peel
Our bed was a mattress on a hard wooden floor
We laughed more than we had ever laughed before
We trekked through the jungle to a deep ravine
And the highest waterfall we had ever seen
We walked through the water flowing over the rocks
There were weird creatures in the water
So we kept on our socks
On the way we saw a python up the tree
It gave us a wink and let us go free
Those days in the jungle were a revelation
It taught us the value of civilisation
What impressed us so was the friendliness of the Thai
When the time came we were sorry to say goodbye.

Nancy Smith

WITCH'S SPELL

Half a brain of living lizard
top it off with a snowy blizzard.
A 30 year old's fungus toes,
make it work with an old hag's nose.
Take a baby rabbit's tail,
mix it in with fingernails.
Kill a shark for its fins,
catch an eagle, use its wings.
Take a couple of spider's legs,
be quick, be quiet, get dragon's eggs.
Pinch of essence of fly's blood,
help it stir, use decaying mud.
Now all you need is a dead pig's ear,
and to finish it off, a cup of fear.

Charlene Soan

IRENE'S BIRTHDAY

It was nice to see you at the Berwick Inn.
There was noise of laughter and quite a din.
We had our delicious meal.
These are memories to seal.
Followed by a bottle of wine
Which was fruity and sublime.
We walked to the Barley Mow.
These days Maman is rather slow.
There was merriment and laughter,
The bill came after.
A year older, a new life doth lease
Irene in Greek means 'peace'.

I T Hoggan

MOTHER LOVE

If I had the power to make wishes come true
Then these are the gifts I'd bestow upon you
Gently, all worries I'd sweep from your mind
Inner peace like a treasure is what you would find
The stars and the moon would be laid at your feet
You would tread a bright path 'til life's span was complete
Good health and the strength to enjoy each new day
With joy in your soul to lighten you way
I would grant you the time to stop and to see
A primrose in spring, a bird in a tree
I would give you the wonders that money can't buy
And a heart full of love 'til the day that I die.

Janet Petchey

NO FUTURE FOR MAN

No future for mankind,
But why should there be?
Pursuit of power and wealth
Is the only game he can see.

He may give to the poor,
Though, not very much.
He thinks they are lazy
And complain far too much.

But when trouble hits him
His true nature shows.
But life never was fair.
It's only now that he knows.

'Why me?' He keeps crying.
'I've striven hard to get on.'
Not one thought for those,
That he trampled upon.

What is it about man,
With his heart full of greed,
Can't he see we must share,
Nature's soil, and its seeds?

No point in expecting
That mankind will progress.
He has savaged the planet
And left the world in a mess.

Not intelligent enough
To use the gift of his birth
If not killing his neighbour,
He is raping the Earth.

John Troughton

My Favourite Place

The place most close to me
Is Meon shore by the sea
It was here I learned to swim
I had to, my brothers threw me in

It is a lovely spot on the Solent beach
Always, lovely always in reach
My brother, friend and I spent days on end
Hoping the fun would never end

My sons love this beach too
Finding plenty of things to do
Collecting cockles and digging in the sand
Getting ice cream from the little van

Today they walk their dog
On a beach that has been there so long
It is my first stop on new year's day
I cannot start the new year in any other way.

Jean Bradbury

WHIZZING ABOUT THE MULBERRY TREE

Oh tale of grace and puppy dog hairs,
Lumpwood stove and gravy squares.
Hot roast spuds over labour jokes
I can see why the froggy croaks.
Rivet, rivet, rivet my girl
Curly Whirly, round and pearl.
Sneaked in preview, upon bear hugs bespoke
Wondrous from a dream awoke.
In morning creaking springs do move
For love within, for love to prove.
And there's more to life than coaching bees
When secrets are truly a gentle squeeze.

Anthony Rosato

THE RELUCTANT HERO

Three mice sat in a corner chewing corn
Down in the earth it was warm, warm, warm,
One mouse looked up slowly and said
'I think our brave Fredy must be dead,
He went out over two or three hours ago
And where he went I think we all know,
Down to the barns to restock our larder
No one but no one could try harder.'

'He may be fine' said another with a sob
'Anyway who's going to take that job?
I can't go I'm expecting our little brood
And we're desperate now for some more food,
You two will have to draw, each one a stick,
Who will lose? Whom will the reaper pick?'

'It's not so bad, you just have to take great care
Make sure you have looked just everywhere,
Avoid the cat, the dog and the mousetraps
Then you should make it safely back, perhaps.'
'I'll go' said mouse three and stood up to leave
'No, no, you can't go, not you, no, no, please.
We'll just sit here and wait just another hour.'
'No, I'm going now just after this shower.'

'You have to take chances and live life each day
Don't worry I'll come back, won't run away,'
'Well good luck then, I'll come part of the way
Up the hill till you're safe in the hay,'
'Shh, listen what is that awful, horrible sound
Like something dead being dragged along the ground,
It's him with a great, huge bundle of hay,
Damn, I'll have to stay in now and put it away.'

Irene Roberts

RETIRED PEDAGOGUE

Grow long your fingernails and cling to life;
Ignore the aching of your weary day
To turn away the sharp edge of the knife.

Forget your family, and the churning strife
That blasts the distant fields of joy away;
Grow long your fingernails and cling to life.

Forget the seasons when the frosts were rife;
Juggle equations to the heart's dismay
To turn away the sharp edge of the knife.

Reject the shrilling nerve-strings of your wife
That shriek at you in age's mad display -
Grow long your fingernails and cling to life.

Beat time to commonsense's drums and fife;
Burn sentiment with dross and love with hay
To turn away the sharp edge of the knife.

Turn off the lamps and gaze into the night,
Lament the darkness of the soul's decay.
Grow long your fingernails and cling to life
To turn away the sharp edge of the knife.

John H Hope

LOST TIME

Tick-tock sounds the clock
As time moves ever on,
The years have passed quickly
Where has my life gone?

Tick-tock goes the clock
The minutes rush quietly by,
The hours turn into days
Coming with barely a sigh.

Tick-tock echoes the clock
It's back against the wall,
Ask questions about life's being
No answer heard at all.

Tick-tock whispers the clock
Hands searching for my fate,
Hell or Heaven are waiting
Time will not keep me late.

Tick-tock sounds the clock
As time moves on regardless
It's for everyone and no one
To fight against it is useless.

Tick-tock says the clock
By day and by night,
Death will call on you
If your time is right.

George S Johnstone

I CANNOT SINK

My dearest love, I need you near to me,
I would be lost if we were torn apart;
When storms and tempests rage upon life's sea,
I hold you close within my fearful heart:
When towering waves blot out all sight of land,
I cannot sink if you will hold my hand.

Life holds no terrors with you by my side,
I have no certainty apart from you;
I find within your arms a place to hide,
Whatever else proves false, your love is true:
When everything around is shifting sand,
I cannot sink if you will hold my hand.

It is my joy to know that we are one,
When all around is bitterness and strife;
When dark, oppressive clouds obscure the sun,
My love, you are my light, you are my life:
Though there may be no certain place to stand,
I cannot sink if you will hold my hand.

Peter English

FRIENDS

Friends are people you meet on the way.
Some just disappear, others tend to stay.
Friends can last forever and a day
Friends are people we cannot do without
How sad if you haven't got friends about
They can make you laugh, bring joy into your life
Your best friend can even be your husband or wife.
Some of my friends I met a long time ago
They ask me a favour and I can say no
No offence is taken and no offence is meant
That is why good friends are sent not lent.
If you have good friends treat them with care
Because one of these days they won't be there.
They'll be gone, then it will be too late
To say 'Thank you, friend, you were my best mate.'

Ennis Nosko-Smith

LOOKING TO THE FUTURE

The proposal

The young man went on bended knee and to his girl he said,
'I fancy you an awful lot and think that we should wed.'
The girl, she was a comely lass, but worldly wise was she,
She thought, he talks of love and wedding rings,
But it's a man laid plot, the aim to get me in his cot.

The young man guessed her consternation and promptly said,
'I mean it, I'll shout it loud to all the nation, and I'll ask your dad.'
'Don't do that,' the young girl cried, 'my dad, he's very staid,
Besides, it's nothing to do with him, 'tis I should feel afraid.'

'Twas then she thought both long and hard (at least a minute)
And she simpered and blushed, how well it suited;
His love he's truly proffered,
I'm getting on now, twenty-one, and no one else has offered . . .
And so the ground was set.

Getting Dad's blessing

So, on his bike, the young man sped,
And with all his charm, his views he spread;
Dad gave his answer and his daughter's hand.
He didn't mention that he thought it grand,
No longer the need to wait up late
To hear the slam of the garden gate,
And know that his daughter was safely home
No need for him the dark, drab streets to comb.

The wedding preparations

The month was quite easy and the bride set the date.
Then came the problems.
Top hat and tails or t-shirt and jeans?
Very posh meals or toast and baked beans?

Whom do we ask and who to leave out?
Family for sure, of that there's no doubt,
Friends bring a problem for of these there are many,
And no way at all can we ask that man Benny.
We must just accept there are those we'll offend.
Shall we sneak off alone as is the new trend?

The bridegroom despaired, was really downhearted,
He said to the girl, 'If I'd known of this fuss
We wouldn't have started.'
At last it was settled and the way ahead clear,
The bride chose her gown, and the bridesmaids selected,
The mums thought real hard of what they should wear,
And the dads settled bills with a pseudo carefree air.

Part two is now in progress.

Edgar Wall

THE CIRCUS CLOWN

Have you ever seen a circus clown, their audience entranced?
Did you ever look behind their mask and wonder if by chance
They are so very different to maybe you or me
Or is it just a clever act for all the world to see?
Did you ever want to find a hole and climb inside to hide,
Or did you wear a public face to hide your fears inside?

Do you ever wish you were the same, circus clowns apart?
Do you ever feel such loneliness clutching at your heart?
Do you ever seek to comfort and make allowance too
In case some other person, feels just the same as you
Or do you tell yourself instead, that people passing by
Are really very confident and can't possible be shy?

Have you considered for a moment, circus clowns aside
That ever single person has doubts deep down inside
But some of us are very good at creating an impression
And we wouldn't want the whole world to see
Beneath our brave expression

Do you ever stop to ask yourself which shyness is the worse
The sort that's quiet and obvious or the noisy extrovert
And have you ever noticed how people can be cruel
And wondered about their motives as they judge and ridicule
I've asked myself these questions but it hasn't done much good
Perhaps we are like the clown, happy, sad or just misunderstood.

Sue Ilsley

MY AUNTIE ADA

From my birth one hot June day
As Grandad's dinnertime whistle blew
He came home and look me, one hour old, up the lodge's way.

My grandparents' room, where I was born
Overlooked the field where the lodges lay
And where from my mother I was roughly torn.

My three young aunts stood in awe,
My face was so disfigured;
A bloody, ugly face they saw, all cut about and raw.

It was my youngest aunt of 13 years
In spite of what she saw
From that day, all her life, she smoothed away my cares.

Up the drive, her black-bowed ringlets bouncing
Adoring, unsteadily I trailed behind.
Her beautiful voice was romantic and entrancing.

Escaping an unquiet house, in fog or rain
I'd cycle to their peaceful home
Many a mile to be with that family again.

She bore a daughter when I was 13
I went to their house to stay.
To her little girl a second mum I've been.

All those have been dead for many a year,
Loving David is still here.
Giving comfort, both mourning that family dear.

Alice Hall

THE PATH OF TIME

Along the path of time I wander
Where no other feet have been
Vivid pictures, lovely colours
Painted there on memory's screen.

Picking mushrooms early morning
With the dew still on the ground
Sparkling cobwebs on the hedges
Quiet, peaceful, not a sound.

Then with basket overflowing
Up the lane we wend out way
There the wandering hens are laying
Underneath the hedge of may.

Birds are singing, greet the morning
With the most melodies sound
God his precious gifts abounding
Here for all, just look around.

Kathleen Fox-Watson

GIBBET HILL

A blustery wind, wild rushing clouds, and glimpses of the sun,
The sort of day my dog and I enjoy a country run.
This pleasant land, this feel free land, its lanes and rights of way
Are all we need, two odd, old friends, to make a pleasant day.
Up Hungerford lane, past steers lot, and on to Gibbet Hill.
We hang about, no pun is meant! I find the view a thrill.
And Buttons wanders back and forth to follow rabbit trails,
If one pops out she pricks her ears and wags her shaggy tail.
We have a love, both she and I, for every living thing
And to this once so wretched place, we hope that love to bring.
This lonely place, this rugged place, its rocks and scanty grass,
This place where we can step aside and let the world go past,
A troubled world, divided world where love has lost its way,
For only when God's love abounds, will peace have come to stay.

Alan Ellsmore

WEST WITTERING

When winter days are dank and grey
My mind will wander
To sandy beaches and sea spray.

To the gentle days of June
Damp ridged sand
And lazy walks on shifting dune.

On the field the kites all fly
Children tugging at the string
Vibrant shapes against the sky.

Families hidden behind windbreaks
Picnic on the grass
With aromatic drifting smoke, from barbecued steaks.

The long yellow beaches, peppered with folk
Building sandcastles
Splashing, paddling and swimming breast stroke.

At five o'clock they go home for tea
Leaving West Wittering
To the seagulls and the sea.

So on dark and drear winter days
I can escape
And dream of my holidays.

Valerie Coleman

A Magic Place, The Lake District

Last night I went for a walk and gazed up to the sky,
The sheer beauty and wonder of it I couldn't deny.
As I watched the setting sun, shine its glow onto the lake,
Such colour and splendour only God in his Heaven could make.
I climbed up the hills, what a wonderful sight,
The mountains, the trees, what a beautiful night.
You can feel the peace in your very soul,
It renews you, gives strength, makes you whole.
I am sad to go, it's been such pure bliss,
The breathtaking beauty and splendour I'll surely miss.
I'll think about it, and dream of it, and hope to come back,
It will sustain me when I'm tired, give me the strength that I lack.
All good things have to end, I'm sorry to say,
But it's been so lovely, I have so enjoyed this stay.

Barbara Ann Barker

THE HOUSE WITH WHITE SHUTTERS

What dreams are these that steal the night
A little house with shutters white,
A door that's always open wide
And someone keeping out of sight.

The summer flowers are white and pink,
A gate leads to the woods I think,
The sycamore gives welcome shade,
A pool where badgers come to drink.

The table's set for scones and tea,
There's someone by the fire I see,
I think I know who it may be
Who nightly shares my dreams with me.

Alice Rawlinson

ADVENTURES OF A PENNY

Mister Penny, where have you been
How many faces and sights have you seen?
Have you travelled on water as well as on land,
Have you travelled in pockets, purses and hand?

Have you visited Scotland, Ireland and Wales
Have you seen the high mountains and low Yorkshire Dales?
Have you sped along highways and wandered down lanes
In cars and on buses, on bikes and in trains?

Have you seen Buckingham Palace - maybe even the Queen
Been on the underground and in London parks green?

And how many faces, white, yellow and brown
Some that are smiling and some with a frown.
Some that are young and some that are old
Some that are shy and some that are bold?

Oh I *do* wish I could travel like you must have done
An adventure like you had would be such great fun!

E Marcia Higgins

INAUDIBLE WORDS OF THE HEART

A perfect start to a perfect day when I laid my eyes upon you
Your smiling eyes washed over me, I knew that was my cue
And so it started, long awaited, a dream to be discovered
As each day passed I found out there was more to be uncovered
Quickly we fell deeper in love, the magic of your power
I wanted to hear your every whisper at every wonderful waking hour
So carefully I listened, then I heard the unspeakable words of our hearts
Lost in the surges of our passion, I knew I had to play my part
We were always on a natural high, our bonded souls carefree
I thrived on all the love and excitement which you gladly
                                        showered on me
So much to give and so much to learn, how could I want for more?
Then one day the angels came, and I was left weeping at the door
Deeper I fell into a hole, the feelings for being suffocated
I had to live through each day, each moment of which I hated
How do you separate two bonded hearts, especially ours so stubborn
Stuck in the middle of two worlds, either way in which I was to be torn
Swept away back to my world to have to start over again
Each day faced with heartache in my tortured heart of pain
And as time slipped by I no longer knew just what was expected of me
After all we were supposed to live in love ever after happily
Safely kept within my heart forever locked away in my past
I loved and lost such a treasure, what more could I possibly ask?
So here I am back on this Earth trying to make a new start
And if I listen carefully, I can hear the inaudible words of your heart.

Nicola Mann

SEASIDE

The rich and lingering smell of salty air,
Blows away any remaining care,
Breathe in deep; delicious, clean air, so sweet,
Shells, seaweed and pebbles crunch under your feet,
Fleeting footprints in the wet sand,
Remains of castles made by a small hand,
Will, in a while be washed away,
Only the smooth shoreline is here to stay.
Pitted timbers rest along the shore,
Mangled objects are strewn across the sandy floor,
Seagulls screech and clamber for picnic remains,
From mussels to chips or discarded ice cream cones.
Trawlers bob on the horizon catching fish,
Cafés wait for the catch to turn into a tasty dish,
The pleasure the seaside gives, lifts our spirits so high,
Maybe, we can soar on the wings of the birds in the sky.

Paula Loveridge

A HOSPITAL FRIENDSHIP

Richer am I for having known you,
And though our paths cross not again,
Yet in my mind's eye, still I see you
Remembering the parting, that brought such pain.
But if for a while, I made you smile,
With some foolish or funny remark,
You alone were the only one,
To know I was 'whistling in the dark'.
Your gentle smile, that all the while,
Says, we're not finished why,
They may send us home
But still we'll roam, Taurus and Gemini!

M Taylor

HOP PICKING

In the summer with Mum we went hopping
And I don't mean up and down on one leg
We were lucky we went home every night
But some stayed on the farm in a shed.
A lorry would come round in the morning
To take us all to the farm
So many of us squashed in that lorry
Pulling us up inside by the arm.
There was not much comfort in that lorry
Hard seats and a tarpaulin on top
I wondered how many more can you get in a lorry
Every five minutes for people he would stop.
I think it was more luck than judgement
That we ever managed to arrive
I think the driver was called Speedy
Because no more faster could he drive.
We walked out to the hop field
And we went to a row with a bin
There we stopped all day long
Trying to fill the bin to the brim.
Sometimes ladies would go missing
Right up to the top of the row
When they came back I would ask them
But they would never tell me where they go.
Up and down the rows I would play
Under the shade of the hops I could be seen
And when I sat down to have a rest
I found out where them ladies had been.

Barry G Randall

MY HOME

My home is my safe place,
Where no one hurts me.
It's the only place where
I want to be.

It may not be flashy,
Or filled with expensive things.
But when I'm at home, it makes
My heart sing.

I find it so cosy and homely,
For all.
When I get visitors,
They're welcome to all.

My kids fill with laughter.
Some joy, and some pain.
But I'll stay in my safe place
And never move again.

So when I grow old, and my body
Wears out
In a wooden casket, they'll carry
Me out.

So to my children, my safe place
Will go.
And to my husband, that I love
So.

Mary George

LUCKY ME

Champagne to me, are my grandsons.
Popping up here and there.
Full of fun and laughter
And plenty of bubble to spare.
Bursting with fizz and exuberance
My life full of remembrance.
Not many are blessed with a family like me
Who welcome their gran, take her out on the spree.
Now that I've reached the twilight of years
So lucky am I with a family who cares.

Jacqueline Bartlett

SMILE

Smile away,
Smile all day,
A smile can chase away the blues
As long as you can too.
Smile a little, smile a lot
Smile with all you've got.
Free that smile all round your face
And reflect it on the human race
Maybe they will smile back at you
And maybe they'll be very glad too.

S Smith

SERENDIPITY

I was sitting on the bench in the churchyard,
under the old knarled yew,
its branches like a giant umbrella,
that the evening sun filtered through.
The sound of the silence, so silent,
no breeze and nothing stirred,
and what was rather disquieting,
there wasn't a sound of a bird.
I sensed a movement around me,
and felt, I was no longer alone,
my curiosity fixed me rigid,
as if I had turned to stone.
It seemed someone had lit a great candle,
wild flowers in abundance shone,
the daisies, who are the eyes of the world,
unamazed, just looked on.
It appeared the past had come to meet me,
there, before my eyes,
a merry band of will-ó-the-wisps,
of every shape and size,
had come to dance the night away,
until the morning sunrise.
For whatever their past may have been,
in our world they've left behind,
to them is now just a dream,
their part played, on the stag of mankind.
I had this longing to join in the fun,
but I knew it wasn't to be,
until my time in this world, was, fully run,
then, only then, could I return, to serendipity.

Audrey Packman

NEVER REPLACED - NEVER FORGOTTEN

Your dark brown hair,
Your big brown eyes,
A radiant smile
That lit up the skies
Someone who always cared,
All those years we spent together,
All the memories we shared.

You don't realise that you not being here makes me blue
Yet no one around even has a clue
To wake up each day: paint on the smile
And live a life on my own for a while.

I look around and see you there
If only you knew how much I care
Wherever I go, whatever I do
I always seem to think of you.

Now there's a place I can keep you near
Remembering the past with many a tear
A place I know you'll never depart
Locked up tight inside my heart.

Maria Jenkinson

STRENGTH TO AMERICA

September the 11th, 2001 was a very black day,
So many lives lost, so much disarray.

America will be stronger and together you'll stand,
With God by your sides with a helping hand.

The tears will cease, but the grief is there,
And at certain moments there will be despair.

You will be in a place where your loved one once stood
And the memories flood back . . . if only I could.

You'll kiss their memory and imagine their face,
And know they're in a beautiful place.

You'll be at their side one of these days,
But I think they know . . . you'll love them always.

A J Witherington

THE FUTURE IS IN THE PAST

When being alone gets intolerable and everything is going wrong,
And the urge to do something drastic is getting very strong,
I just think of you, and a warm glow spreads all over me,
I don't need pills and potions when I'm down - you are my remedy.
When I recall your beauty, it seems like my duty,
To write some elegant prose,
You bring out the bard within me, and my poetical ability overflows,
Lazing in my hammock in the shade of the old walnut tree,
Fond memories come flooding back to how we used to be.
Laying here just reminiscing on this long, warm summer day,
Of all the wonderful times we had, and why you went away.
I remember when we first met, and that feeling I had inside,
And the thrill from just seeing you, was so very hard to hide.
The colour of your hair, the trendy clothes you wear
    Your smile so exciting,
I notice you looking at me, and the sparkle in your eyes was
                         so inviting.
I held you tight, the feeling was right, your perfume captured my senses
The way you looked, I was hooked, you broke down all my defences.
Our first kiss was sheer bliss, I've never yet had one like it,
So passionate and warm, we blew up a storm, I think you
                    must be psychic.
When I think of all the good times we had, a tingle goes up my spine,
For this feeling I always get, tells me you will always be mine.

Brian Lorkin

NEW YEAR 2002

Is this new year a different one
Or will things be the same?
Will man still abuse the natural world
Or take stock of who's to blame?
Will lessons be learnt from mistakes past made
Or the problems swiftly ignored?
I suspect politicians will still call the tune
That plays to the money assured.
Better the new year a chance to change
Life for the betterment of man
Freeing the people from angered strain
Liberating hearts while we can.
Taking the time to think of others
Making life simpler world-wide
Returning to basics, the core of simplicity
Finding our innermost pride.

Lin Bourne

ME?

I've long blonde hair and big brown eyes
My legs go on forever.
I turn the heads of all the guys
When wearing jeans of leather.

My conversation has no end,
Interesting facts I've plenty.
I've loads of money I can spend
The cupboard's never empty.

I drive so fast, foot flat on the floor,
My racing car is swish.
I could never be a bore,
Me? Oh how I wish!

Carole Wise

THE TELL TALE SIGNS OF AGEING

I wasn't really aware of the changes taking place,
Until I looked in the mirror, at the difference in my face,
I had lines leading everywhere, crows feet beside my eyes,
I could not believe the wrinkles, some were long and some were wide.

My chin was getting bolder, my neck began to sag,
The lines above my lips made a pattern, like a crab,
My forehead had lines above my nose,
There were pink veins on my skin,
The answer has to be a facelift, to get my bits tucked in.

When the day came, I was petrified, as I was put to sleep,
Long hours of surgery, bandages galore,
The new me I was going to meet,
Two weeks went by, the bandages came off, as I looked at myself
I saw, this beautiful person with lovely skin, I will never age no more.

I got dressed up, I hit the town, my new looks were out to score,
I met a man, a lovely man, who walked me to my door,
A few weeks passed by, I was feeling great,
I now had a man in my life,
The one thing he forgot to tell me, he also had a wife.

I was so upset my skin was sore,
I rubbed my eyes until they were raw,
I glanced in the mirror, to my horror I
could see those horrific lines that haunted me,
So may I suggest, don't even moan,
Just grow old gracefully, and leave well alone . . .

Marion Totten

MY SOUVENIR ELEPHANTS

I've been a travelling adventurer, animality's my favourite scene,
Now a souvenir collection is mine from faraway places I've been.
It's not an assembly of knicks and knacks, reflecting wherever I roam,
It's my model collection of elephants
And they're spreading all over my home.
They seem to have characters all of their own,
So I've given them each their own name,
My home is a mini-menagerie zone,
I'm living with little big game.
604, last time I kept score,
Remind me of hot foreign climes,
Where oft I would toddle, collect a new model,
My tropical travelling times:-

Cool elephants cocoon in my kitchen,
Eight others have homes in the hall,
Some swing upside down from the ceiling,
And a weary one waits by the wall,
Two tuskers cavort on the carpet, one ruminates under the rug,
One rests on a rock, two climb on the clock,
And a jumbo just jaunts with a jug.

Wild elephants ride round on my washing machine,
Six others slip under the sink,
Their numbers still grow, and they all seem to go to those places
You just wouldn't think,
Grey elephants gad round in the greenhouse,
Six sheltering down by the shed,
A big bull is based by my bath and bidet,
With a bigger bull basking in bed.

One elephant's head is so glaringly red,
With another's exceedingly blue,
The red will recline in the room where we dine,
But the blue lives alone in the loo,
An elephant stands tall by the rear garden wall,
Others graze by the grey gravel path,
But my favourite of all, is the one that is small,
He's a loofah I use in the bath.

I've an old Indian elephant with only one eye,
And two ears that are covered in rust,
And a powerfully poised pet African bull
In a petrified permanent must!
Six sweet Sri Lankans are scaling the stairs,
Six Kenyans are coming back down,
One elephant smiles, one climbs over stiles,
One carries a sad puzzled frown.

I've a massive Malaysian mad moody big bull
That none of the others are hassle,
And his mauve Maharajah meandering mate,
Multicoloured with blankets and tassel,
I've given these bulls all such butch bullish names,
Just like Elvis and Beckham and Elton,
All their ladies are neat, looking solemn and sweet,
And have tusks that no butter would melt on.

These elephants roam over all my home,
All my rooms have some elephant junk,
So next time I stray to a land faraway,
I'll take care what I pack in my trunk!

Keith Thompson

WALKIES

Dogged by your love
on some small Pennine hill
I strode through grass
the colour of old straw
and laughed that I felt fine.
Yes everything was fine.

Mute in its rib cage
curled my careful heart,
muzzle on paw,
apparently asleep.

Months later, protestations
long since over,
you rearranged the contents
of your car so
I could ride with you.
A single act of care:
you snapped my safety belt.
- Too late, too late!

On the train,
I felt the sudden
straining of the leash
and pulled in vain.

Check your vehicle:
I think my heart is there.

Nancy Cass

SCHMUTTER

The man's an utter nutter:
Why did they set him free?
He can't tell talk from stutter.

Just listen to him mutter,
A bonnet in his bee:
The man's an utter nutter.

Can't help but splat and splutter,
And prattle endlessly:
He can't tell talk from stutter.

Watch him run and scutter,
An ear in his flea:
The man's an utter nutter.

He'll flap along and flutter,
Shout incoherently:
He can't tell talk from stutter.

Buried deep in clutter,
I trust you would agree:
The man's an utter nutter:
He can't tell talk from stutter.

Jim Storr

THE BIRKENHEAD ARGYLE

When you talk with older folk
You always get a smile
Stirring up those memories
About the old Argyle.

Once starred Sir Harry Lauder
This theatre had some style
The Two Tonne Tessie O'Shea
The biggest by a mile.

And if you weren't quite up for it
They'd give you one rough ride
But if you could make them all laugh
They'd go home satisfied.

In these more enlightened times
It may have been preserved
And like the Cavern years ago
No more than it deserved.

When you chat with older folk
You always raise a smile
Now I guess it's far too late
To raise the old Argyle.

John Smurthwaite

DURBAN SHORE

Where India meets Africa
By palm trees lazy sway
Is where we drove and walked a while
On this quite perfect day.

When darkness came we ate and drank
Where millionaires hold sway
The hospitality first class
On this quite perfect day.

Daniel Jack

PLEASE DON'T INTERRUPT ME

I want to tell you something.
I want to tell you how.
I think it is important
And I'd like to tell you now.

So please don't interrupt me.
Please just let me speak.
If you don't let me finish
We could be here all week.

Please don't interrupt me.
It isn't very nice.
Please don't interrupt me.
I don't want to say it twice.

I'm trying hard to tell you.
I'm trying to explain.
But you always interrupt me
You really are a pain.

Don't you know I'm fed up?
Can't you see I'm cross?
Won't you listen to me
While I get this point across?

Now you're certain that you'll listen?
I've been praying for this day.
You've made me truly happy
But I've forgotten what to say.

Brian Thompson

A SHOCKING WAY TO GO

Ten long years
Have passed him by.
Locked in a cell
Just waiting to die.
The time has come
For his last meal
While his lawyer does his best
In one last appeal.
He has just been told
He will die at dawn
As his family say their goodbyes
As they prepare to mourn.
They shaved his arms
His legs and head
Then he asked them for forgiveness
As his prayers were said.
They took him down the corridor
While dragging both his feet
Knowing at the other end
Is that electrifying seat.
As they strapped him in the chair
He screamed out 'Why?
I didn't do it honestly
I don't want to die.'
Above him was a helmet
Which they put upon his head
They turned on all the power
Within minutes, he was dead.

Stephen Hibbeler

Two Songs Of The Road

Melton may be Mowbray
Tho' some call it Constable.
'Tis certainly not as hot
As Redmarley D'Abitôt.

Let's hear it for Hay on the Wye!
The sun always shines from a clear blue sky,
Except when it rains.
Then everyone looks
For second hand books!

G E Carr

A SONG OF THE SIXTIES

Working at the pickle factory isn't any fun:
I only go there mornings, so I can leave at one.
It's not the same for the others, they have to stay till five
Thinking, from Monday to Friday, how they'll ever survive.

Reeking of pepper and mustard, watching the vinegar rise,
Terrible for the complexion, and not good news for the eyes,
We begin the week quite brightly, babbling of discos and bars,
And come home feeling as sour as the stuff that's filling the jars!

M Carr

A VIRUS

If a virus lives within its host
and procreates then dies,
what other tiny living things
beneath the surface lie?
To a virus every living cell
must seem a mighty place,
with all lovely virus comforts
to feed its virus face.
It will not know that its host lives,
nor will it care at all,
so long as it can live its life
and really have a ball.
Perhaps us puny humans
are a virus in God's plan,
and we live our lives, then die again
in an entity like man.
Perhaps we live our lives
inside a strange, but living cell,
inside another living host -
you can never really tell.
We will never know the answer
to the question that I ask.
Are we just a pesky virus
or is mankind here to last?

Walter Christmas

DARKEST DAYS

Where have you gone to my elusive dream?
Deserting me now when I'm needing you most.
Trickling by like a fast running stream,
Fading to darkness like a transparent ghost.
Teasing my mind, pretending all's well,
Giving me false hopes that rapidly fade.
Leaving me lost in this troublesome hell,
Taking my sunshine and giving me shade.
Searching for you gives me sorrow and pain,
Like flames that burn in the pit of my heart.
Leaving its ashes like an ugly stain,
With ease, you are tearing my whole world apart.
Oh, why did you take my contentment away,
Fleeing my thoughts and giving me pain.
Having you once I thought you would stay,
Oh, peace of mind embrace me again!

Neata Todd

CHILDREN

The funny things that children say
Just make me split my sides
I've been with children every day
For most of my busy life.

'Me want to ride a bike' said Joe
No it's 'I want to ride a bike'
'You are too big to have a go'
'Me think so too' said Mike.

'Fish for sale' said a three year old
Grandad took one from the net
He popped it in his mouth so cold
'You can't eat that. It's a pet!'

When making cards for Mother's Day
I explained it's for your mum
Your mum is kind and helps you play
'Don't think so,' said Jake, ''cos she smacks my bum.'

B Gordon

LIFE

Where has it gone, this love of life?
Into the depths of sin and strife?
Are we really sinking, lower each year?
Making the gutter appear sincere!
Sinister it was in my younger days
Didn't want to go there no, no way.
Where has it gone, this love for all?
Making everything seem a huge brick wall.
Has the work we've done, and the hills we've climbed,
Done nothing to prove it after all this time?
With my cataract eyes and limping gait,
I'm not far short of the pearly gates.
So could somebody quick, help my heart to tick
And not have to wait for a screw to slip.
There must be somewhere on this golden Earth,
Where I can sing and laugh with mirth.

B Spinks

SIMPLY YOU
(In memory of Aunt Sheila)

It never, not once, occurred to me
That you would not be around today
And it's so easy to reminisce on certain things you would say
Remembering your laugh and the style that you wore
It pains me that you are no more.
Time was not kind, I hate it for that
Looking through photos of where you once sat
I don't always like to reflect on these sad memories
Nothing makes any sense, no poignant theories
We learn to heal enough to find a different way
And not to feel guilt when we are doing OK.

Karen Langridge

GOSSIP

During the war, it was known
Loose tongues cost lives, so
Before your brain slips out of gear
Think of those you hold dear.

Too much mouth and gossiping
Destroying lives is a sin.
Count to three and hold it in
Learn to stop your gossiping.

One day you'll get your face filled in
Another argument you may not win.
Talk is cheap, consequences devastating
It doesn't make you better in popularity rating.

Hatred, anger from unkind words
Has been linked to suicides.
A one to one and left at that
Leaves no one else to chew the fat.

You will never hold a friend,
If it's everyone's ear you bend
Whispers in the night
Can be an awful sight.

Instruction, guidance or example
Encouragement or telling off, doesn't rankle
Pray God may help you button it
Before on you we all spit.

Rachel Thompson

WONDROUS GRACE

Lord what a wonder of grace
To come and gaze upon your face

To yield all my burdens every day
When I come to you and pray

That in your presence I might dwell
That of your love you may tell

Lord guide me each and every day
That I may live your spirit's way

As I walk the path of life
Amid the pain, the tears and strife

Thank you Lord you keep watch over me
And safely through my troubles see

Thank you Lord for your love divine
May you precious Saviour ever be mine

May I lead others to knowing you
As they see your glory in all I do

Saviour, may your love shine from my face
As I walk daily in you wondrous grace

Ken Lewis

ALONE

Where am I? Where are you?
Can't you see I need someone?
My head is spinning, my legs are weak
Oh! My throat is so dry!
The room is closing in on me, I'm going
To be crushed - my head hurts.
I see the blue sky, no clouds! No rain!
Just the sun and the dry barren earth.
How long have I been here?
A day! A week! A year!
When are you coming home?
Please hurry and help me
If I can just get upstairs get some water
But I can't, my legs will not move,
My mind is saying go - just try, but my body
Is telling me what's the use? He's not
Coming back! It's a lie you will I know
If I can just hold out a little longer
You'll soon be here!
Do I hear footsteps outside? Listen carefully
No it's only me imagining what I want to
Hear! I can't take it any more I can't go on
I'm going to die! No you mustn't, you must
Have faith and just believe.
Wait! What's this? Who's calling?
If I can just get to the door
Please try, slowly, inch by inch
Oh thank God you're here

Jean Lewis

THE KIDS OF TODAY

Oh the kids of today!
You can hear the parents say,
All they do is play music full blast,
Can't they remember they are the kids of the past?

Oh the kids of today!
Well they seem to have their say,
Gone are the days when children should be seen, and not heard,
You can even say they have the last word.

The kids of today!
Are the next future generation,
Sometimes I look and think they don't come up to my expectation,
But then again they are only the kids of today.

The bedroom is a mess, papers, comics on the floor,
'Please keep out' a note on the door,
What ever happened to the golden haired doll, and cute little bear?
If they can't have CD, DVD, PC, it's just not fair.

High fashion trainers on their feet,
Oh, I have just got to compete,
Things are made not to last,
All I can say is I'm glad, I'm a kid of the past.

Rosalind Jennings

MY MUM

My mum is the best,
But I'm the pest,
She is the greatest of all,
I know she's rather tall,
But I'm rather small.

I like my mum for who she is,
She's up and away in a whiz,
She can shout and bellow,
She likes the colour yellow,
And her favourite word is hello.

My mum is very kind,
And sometimes hard to find,
She is as soft as a dove,
This is a poem from high above,
Because my mum's full of love.

Scott Smith (11)

DOMESTIC BLISS

There was a man, came from Stoke
He wasn't a very big bloke.
He got on his bike in the middle of the night
In order his wife to provoke.

His wife said at once, 'I can't have that'
And locked up the house all around,
He soon came back and crept in the cat flap,
The folks all around said his mind wasn't sound.
He crawled into bed and put his hand on her tum
And she kicked him out on his bum.

Fred Simpson

MEMORIES OF A COUNTRY FAIR

Acres of green baked by the sun
Where hundreds of folk came to have fun.
Long lines of stalls displaying their wares
As they had done at previous fairs.

Candyfloss skittles, bowling for pig.
Someone gave rides in an old-fashioned gig.
Further down field they found birds of prey,
Tied to some pegs so they couldn't fly away.

Rides on the donkeys from Hammerwood Road
That didn't seem to mind each differing load.
On to refreshments, 'What's there for tea?'
'I hope there's some left for little old me.'

'Aunt Nellie has lost her little gold watch,'
And, 'Uncle has won a bottle of Scotch.'
The children were happy just being around
With floss and ice cream as they sat on the ground.

At five a lady in tank-top and pants
Had just about sold her flowers and plants.
At six the large field had to be clear,
And was with some shouts of 'See you next year.'

Roger Tremethick

I REMEMBER WITH AFFECTION

'I'll miss you, oh I'll miss you!'
As you held me close that night.
About to part forever,
One kiss, then gone from sight.
For four long years of wartime
We had worked there, side by side.
There grew a bond between us
That both of us denied.
For you, my friend, were married
And faithful to your wife.
But in those years of darkness
We cheered each other's life.
Now the war had ended,
Demobbed and on your way,
One last dance, a hug, a kiss,
And then we had to say:
'I'll miss you, oh I'll miss you!'
As we murmured our goodbye.
I remember with affection,
That kiss, those words, that sigh.

Beryl R Daintree

THE DARKNESS OF LIFE

I have thought of you every day,
Your soft kiss on my cheek,
I dream of seeing you in every way,
I miss you . . . I feel weak.

There's a picture of you in my mind,
I can't believe that you have gone,
Where's the key to your heart I must find?
You are my love . . . the only one.

I can still hear the echo of your voice in my ear,
You released the worry of my eternal fear,
I can still see your tender face,
I lay my head on your resting-place.

I wish I could be with you in God's kingdom,
However, the time is almost here,
When in a bundle of happiness you will reappear.

Soon we will be together . . . this time it's forever.

Enrica Francis

MY STAR

Holding your hand, stroking your head
Lying with you beside your bed.
I prayed for you to stay with me
Though sadly this was not to be.

How selfish was I on that night
Begging, 'Please stay,' I had no right
You gave to me relentlessly
My love now also sets you free.

All of the love plus all the pain
The sacrifice the lack of gain.
Total commitment to the end,
Darling Mother, my truest friend.

The brightest star you'll always be
Your light will always shine for me.
Always an inspiration Ma
My own eternal 'superstar'.

Forever, brightening dull days
Following your footsteps, always.
Working hard to match up to you
And to your memory I'll be true.

Always working, no rest at all,
Labouring on since I was small.
Savour the moment, take it
Mother rest now, having earned it.

Loveliest lady, darling love,
No sweeter soul floating above.
Shine down tonight and evermore
Waiting for me at Heaven's door.

Janet Emery

FAIRY MAIDS

Fairy maid of the fields swaying in the breeze
the Elizabethan serenade wafts through trees.
Fairy souls sing to the tune as they float on gossamer wings
mysteries of the meadow are enclosed by the fairy rings.
Only shown to those children who believe in dreams
as across the meadow, they in sleep do drift it seems.
Pixies play their flutes to take up the mood
while creatures of wild look on from magic wood.
Comes the morn, faces pressed to window
to see if dreams are still in meadow down below.

John Clarke

EDELWEISS

A spray of edelweiss beckoned to me
Just out of reach on the climb I had chosen,
I did want that spray as a buttonhole
Dressed as I was in lederhosen.

I regretted I hadn't taken a companion
As I stood on a crag half-way to my goal,
But I liked to climb with only the cowbells
Of the upper slopes leading to the Tyrol.

As I assessed the distance between
Me and my goal, I unwound my rope against a fall
And belayed myself to the frightening wall
As a sunbeam glanced through the clouds.

It lit up my edelweiss, which became an obsession.
I began to climb, always three point anchored,
And then it happened. 'Dear God' I cried
As I swung out above the valley like a bird.

I dropped and crashed back against the wall
Several feet lower with an almighty bang.
I managed to attach four points again
But this time above the overhang.

I reached the little delicate white flower
And put it where it belonged.
Then I was satisfied with what I had done
And climbed down to the valley whistling a song.

Rosemary Smith

THE VISIT

I sense I have been here before,
When I tap, tap, tap on your door.
You let me in, I look around,
I feel so strange, dim lights, no sound.
No need to speak, I feel the mood,
So strong and yet so subdued.

The place is large in every way,
Restful, calming, no disarray,
A sanctuary or so they say.
I feel so humble when I look around,
A feeling of peace, joy, warmth,
Still no sound.

The windows sparkle like jewels in a crown,
Colours glistening, with figures all around.
I sit and rest my weary bones, on seats so hard,
And beautifully carved.
I don't notice the discomfort while I look around,
At all the beauty I have found.

I feel the urge to stay some more,
But went back out through that door.
I know I will return again,
To visit this beautiful domain.

Olive Hudson

HARVEST JOYS

A random truth is often found in common things that round us lie,
The harvest with its work-filled quest, brings peace and beauty
                                                    to the eye.

From golden corn to purple plum, a treasury of riches pure.
The clustered grape along the vine, the luscious pear a constant lure.

The peach along the sun-drenched wall, berries sweet and stoned
                                                    fruit sour,
Nectarines, cherries, apricots, the ripened fruit in apple bower.

The maize that stands so straight and tall; peas, potatoes,
                                        beans and beet,
The hops that dance along the bine, each to its season, cold and heat.

Marrow, melon, mustard, mint, carrots, onions, chive and cress,
Sunflower, linseed oilseed rape, yield their oil beneath the press.

We gather in with thankful heart, another harvest takes its bow.
Granary filled and hay barn high, then seedtime beckons
                                        with the plough.

Norma B Rudge

Working Together

My husband and I have two gardens,
One at the front and one at the back,
So we work together and really do not slack.
To grow out vegetables and flowers
Unless the rain comes down in showers
Then the sky is looking very very black.
But we really need some rain
And my husband makes it plain
Or the plants they would not grow
For he often tells me so.
So we get on well together
And never mind the weather
In the bungalow where we have lived
For seventeen years.

P M Dunn

LOOKING BACK ON ONE'S FUTURE

When I look back on future's threat to me
Which has not manifested anything so bad,
I wonder why it was not plain to see
There was so little reason to be sad.
All hopes and fears have only temp'ral stay
With the small, encompassed world of thought;
Yet stop us achieving what we might have sought
By wasting precious hours of life away.
Why can't our elders pass this wisdom down,
Surrounded as they've been with futile fears?
They could prevent us sensing years of woe
Trapped in some tiny cell-like living throe.
Oh give us all the gift to wait and see
Futures far better than they seemed to be.

Keith Collins

ANGEL AT MY SIDE

I have many special pencils; they all seem to write for me
I was given this gift from God for everyone to see.
Words, rhymes just enter my head
At my side is an angel
Can you guess what he said?
'You are not able to see me, but I am always near
My hand on your cheek
To take away a tear,
My hand in yours to dispel any fear.
I kiss you on the cheek at night
And hold you when you wake with fright.
I smile with you when you're happy
Cry when you are sad
I always give you hugs
I've lost count of the ones you have had
I am always there to hold you
I often whisper in your ear
I wish that you could hear me
When I clap and cheer.
People often see me, as I am a part of you
People see our caring nature
They all have angels too.
Your friends have been picked
With so much time and care
They are the ones
That will always be there.'
So this is what my angel said
With the pencil that I hold
Somewhere there is a message
More valuable than gold.

N J Isherwood

THE SCHOOL TRIP

Can't sleep at night I toss and turn
Can't face a meal it makes my stomach churn
I'm a nervous wreck need to get a grip
My son has gone away on his first school trip
I ironed his clothes and packed his bag
Gave him instructions and tried not to nag
Don't forget to shower, brush your teeth, comb your hair
And change your dirty clothes, socks and underwear
Do as you are told and don't wander off
Wrap up warm so you don't get a cough
Don't stay awake chatting late into the night
No sneaking out of bed giving the teachers a fright
But do have fun as you spread your wings
Enjoy all the adventures that growing up brings
But our house is too quiet when you are not around
Can't wait till you're home Son safe and sound

Jackie Manning

FRIENDS

Everyone has days of sadness
When worries fill your head
And money that you've saved for fun
Has gone on bills instead.
Why waste your days on worry?
Why fill your time with dread?
Sit back, relax, consider
The things you have instead.
The sun, the moon, the stars
The flowers, birds and trees
The laughter of a child
Such wondrous gifts are these.
Health and strength are blessings
On which happiness depends
And the greatest gift of all
Are dear and trusted friends.

Jean O'Donogue

THE DESERT

The chilly night air pervades the desert land.
The sand I lie upon coarse grained and wild.
So different from that finer type of sand
From seashore, that I played on as a child.

I shiver, and it's not because the temperature is low.
But my confidence is failing, and I find
So many mixed emotions in all my actions show,
As a hundred themes of terror plague my mind.

Then sparkling stars in the dark mantle seen
Relieve my tensions, as I lie down to rest.
Slow into sleep I drift, into a welcomed dream
And in the lonely night, my fears confess.

I see in dream, the water gushing from a spring,
High on a mountainside, covered in mist.
To see it turn into a torrent, tumbling
And on its way each stony outcrop kissed.

And then a river wide and deep revealed
Whereon the sunlight sparkles like a gem.
Or in a narrow canyon is concealed
Hidden from the sight of mortal men.

The desert that is in my soul, has brought
A yearning that through all of time has trod.
To find the source of 'living water', I have sought.
Discovering its only source is found, in God!

Dennis Brockelbank

RIVERS OF TEARS

No more the meadows green with scented wild flowers,
No mushroom rings to sit in to while away the hours.
The wild flowers have all been destroyed,
And is now a colourless void.

The lapwing that twisted and weaved, and let out a shriek,
To protect their nests from people's feet.
The sky lark that flies in a clear blue sky
And sings on the wing is now a far off cry.

Frogs that laid their eggs in a shallow pond,
Have all gone because they couldn't adapt.
The snipe that used to dive, with wings that hum.
They have all gone now, with the setting sun.

I look into the water from a lonely river bank,
Where two rivers meet no life meets anymore.
No more will our rivers run with clean fresh water,
There will only be rivers of tears.

When the sun goes down for the last time,
There will be no eyes to see it set.
No memories for you or me, no memories to forget,
At the last hazy sunset.

Philip Randall

A BLESSED LIFE

As I look back over my life, which has passed like a shooting star
leaving a trail of memories filled with love and adventure.
Travels to foreign lands, Bosnia, Vietnam, Belize
climbing live volcanoes and diving coral seas.

I've been loved by my family, taught the value of a smile
the gift of a friendship, that will withstand the mile.
To be easy with all animals, notice the breath of spring,
the beauty in a day break, a kestrel on the wing.

I've been honoured to meet people, from such differing walks of life,
both those born into privileged lives, and into poverty or strife.
I've witnessed determination and the strength to carry on,
seen the humble side of royalty, great courage in the young.

I've now come to a pause, where I'm feeling so content,
I have lived out all my dreams, have no regrets of time I've spent.
I've been blessed with a love, that will burn strong 'til I die,
Through whatever lies ahead, with my best friend by my side.

I thank you Lord for blessing me, with such a life as this,
help me be to worthy, of this contented bliss.

Sophie Moran

A VERY CORNY TALE

On my foot there's a lump.
Is it? . . . You know . . . or just a harmless bump.
Perhaps amputation right up to the hip,
But first for pathology a tiny little snip.

First check my insurance is all up to date.
I shan't be here for the church summer fete,
Will leave my body to medical school
Must stop this moaning, I'm a silly old fool.

Doctor said, 'Just a corn, no need to worry,'
Felt so embarrassed I left in a hurry
Dashed out of the surgery in a terrible rush
And got squashed quite dead by a No. 10 bus.

M M Kostiuk

WHEN YOU WAKE UP

When you wake up in the morning do you wonder what's in store?
Do you think you'll have a good day as you go out through the door?
As you hurry to the bus stop, are you on your way to work
Or are you going shopping, on the corner do you lurk?
As you look into your shopping bag have you got your shopping list
And do you start to grumble as you see the bus you missed
Go on its way without you, do you just walk home instead
And wish that it was night-time so that you can go to bed?
No, you carry on regardless and walk down to the mall
As you ride up on the escalator you meet up with a pal.
You sit and have a cup of tea and start to simmer down
Then you go about your shopping as you walk around the town.
It's time to head for home again, you feel much better now
The shopping's done, you've bought a treat, the frown's
                                        gone from your brow,
When day is done you go upstairs and on your bed you lay
And think about tomorrow, but tomorrow is another day.

Jean M Skitrall

IVORY TOWER TERZANELLE

Rose lived up in an ivory tower,
Surrounded by skies where swallows flew.
How did she spend each locked-away hour?

There was no blot on the horizon - spoiling the view.
Like a hermit or nun she lived secluded,
Surrounded by skies where swallows flew.

Look down on the world, you're so deluded.
Downstairs and outside - this loner wouldn't go.
Like a hermit or nun she lived secluded.

Walrus and narwhal tusks trapped the sunset's glow.
Nobody can touch her or disturb her there.
Downstairs and outside - this loner wouldn't go.

Did she sit combing lazy-blonde hair?
Its secret windows were one-way glass.
Nothing can touch her or disturb her there.

Lost in a reverie of better-days passed,
Rose lived up in an ivory tower.
Its secret windows were one-way glass.
How did she spend each locked-away hour?

Mark Young

GLORIOUS PRINCES STREET

Princes St, oh Princes St,
So lovely and so unique?
What are the planners trying to do now
Turn you into some ultra modern freak?
Will the 'powers that be' never learn from past mistakes
And instead of radical change
Making the very best of what is within range
Not destroying what can never be replaced
History and national pride?
Where are all the pioneers who worked for the good of the people
And had pride in their trade?
Not international companies and entrepreneurs
Making money and having power over the underpaid.
When tramways, suburban railways, etc
Were phased out and the potential
Of the canals and waterways ignored
The future wasn't considered
And what could take place.
All the congestion of traffic and streets as is seen today
Has happened because the 'powers that be'
Got their own way.
Now no one seems to really care
And power and greed has become the first need!
Where are all the good leaders
Who can stand on their own feet
And not just think of their parliamentary seat?
Withstanding pressure from incoming companies
And giving in to their greed.
Although competition and progress there will always be
It doesn't mean that we have to build as high as we can
And dig down very deep
Spoiling the beauty of landscape and demolishing
What we can never retrieve.

Just to be upsides with some ultra modern cities
And be one of the 'elite'
Instead of making the very best of potential
Down our own street!
Everyone and everything is unique
And we should all treasure and protect
What is worthy of 'keep'!
Long live and bless our dear Princes St!

J W Wight

THE NIGHT

The lingering night caresses the sweet scented grass
As she lovingly wraps her dark mantle o'er the earth.
Softly she steals through shady forests
Spreading her soft touch amongst the trees
Bringing sleep to the flowers and leaves
Gracefully she encompasses the mighty mountains
Till their silvery sides dim from their height
And her shadows bid the valley 'goodnight'.

'Oh people,' she sighs, 'so rarely do you see
Such beauty before you.
For in the light, you do rush and toil
But to the night you close your eyes
Here is where tranquillity lies!
Raise your furrowed brows and look at me.
Still is my air, quiet is my voice.
Be at peace in your hearts and calmly rejoice.'

Serenely she waltzes o'er the meadows
Smilingly she beholds the owl
And all the other creatures who share her delight.
The river murmurs in pleasure
As she strides across with leisure
To the world beyond;
Along the pathway of bliss
She turns to the moon and blows a kiss.

Angela Cookson

SHED NO TEARS

Oh dear! Alas! O lack-a-day!
My bloody shed has blown away.

Jill, Jill, come quick, come here, do hurry.
The flaming thing's halfway to Surrey.

(I think the Lord is on your side
He knew that shed was my joy and pride.)

It flew right past two strolling clerics
Who stared and said 'Dear God! That's Eric's.'

A UFO expert cried 'That's good.'
'It's the first I've seen that's made of wood.'

A builder mused 'The roof's not filled in.
Perhaps it is a listed buildin'.'

A voice from Heaven spake 'No excuse,
Get thee some planks of pine and spruce

A bag of nails, some panes of glass
Mark thee a plan out on the grass

Dig deep and make a good strong base
Now bolt thy new shed into place

Come snow or rain or fire or hail
Your new 'gazebo' should not fail.'

God moves in some mysterious ways
At least that's what the Bible says

It must be true, I'm sure it's reet
But you'd think He'd watch where He put His feet!

Roy Smith

SEPTEMBER 11TH

I looked upon the face of hell
  Of grief and sadness I could tell.
I looked upon the face of shame
  It turned towards the wall again.
I looked around for happiness
  Simplicity of life I guess.
But the face that looked right back at me
  Was that of pure misery.
Of hope that's lost, of grief that's been
  Of completely shattered dreams.

A single tear took a destined route
  It lingered then it fell
It carried with it any hope the future had to sell.
  I'd like to say that this was but a small deviance from the rhyme
That the face of happiness will always rule sublime.
  But I am a realist in this changing time.

Yet then I looked and saw the face of hope and charity
  They both with such a kindly smile were looking back at me.
Then I saw a quirky grin from faith
  Who said, 'We are not beaten yet.'
I felt the power of these words and took another step.
  But then I heard revenge arrive. I felt it time to run and hide
Be careful, hate will hitch a ride
  Not caring who's left to survive.
Sorrow looked so forlorn
  It knew revenge had just been born.

A Seago

ME

When I entered this world, I wasn't very old,
A sweet little angel! Or so I've been told,
Plodding along life's highway, half-hearted, sometimes impassive,
Sometimes without hope, enthusiasm or initiative,
I've gathered many memories, had my fair share of knocks,
Mentally bruised and battered, like the sea against the rocks

Ambition; just a word; as the years rolled gently by,
Fields of dreams were languid, never reaching for the sky,
Strolling past each milestone, phlegmatic, never sporty,
Until there came the turning point, I'd reached the age of forty!
A giant rock exploded, leaving fragments all around,
Each one with a purpose, bedded in my mind to drown!
To release them to the surface, I had to learn to swim,
Studied for a grade, the brain cells really aren't that dim!
Confirmed myself a Christian, cleansed the spirit and the soul,
Flew across the Atlantic! To the King of Rock and Roll!
Dabbled with the technical, another grade I've passed!
Mirror; signal; manoeuvre, learned to drive at last!

Particles of rock in the seabed of my mind,
Rising to the surface, the rights of which I've signed,
To be published in a book! Chapter, song and verse,
Fingers strumming music . . . concentrate! . . . Rehearse!
My road of life has opened up, new ventures at each bend,
Fantasies and daydreams; living out until the end!

Jan Hall

TAMMY

Tammy was my special friend
Her loving nature knew no end
She sensed my mood, my up and down
When I was sad she'd act the clown.

Together we'd walk on days so pleasant
Espying the deer, rabbits or pheasant
She'd take the lead and make the pace
Judging it all by the look on my face.

The joy she felt was clear to see
As she bounced around with jollity
Her whole existence made for fun
No time had she for feeling glum.

In quiet times she'd sit with me
Listening to music or watching TV
Happy to be at peace by my side
Always my friend, my chum, my guide.

We had a bond, an affinity
I loved her and she loved me
We said it often in our different ways
Over the years and months and days.

It broke my heart one Easter day
When I was told she'd passed away
No more to hear that welcome bark
To feel a wet nose in the dark.

The big brown eyes once bright and clear
Closed in death, no longer here
But I must be grateful that I had some time
With this glorious, ebullient, effervescent canine.

She wasn't my dog, she belonged elsewhere
I was a visitor, a dog sitter there
So I thank the fates that said she'd be
My special friend who gave love to me.

Kathleen Marshall

THE GOLDEN CHAINS OF FRIENDSHIP

Friendship is a golden chain,
The links are friends so dear,
And like a rare and precious jewel
It's treasured more each year . . .
It's clasped together firmly
With love that's deep and true,
And it's rich happy memories
And fond recollections, too . . .

Time cannot destroy its beauty
For as memory lives,
Years can't erase the pleasure
That the joy of friendship gives . . .
For friendship is a priceless gift
That cannot be bought or sold,
But to have an understanding friend
Is worth far more than gold . . .
And the golden chain of friendship
Is a strong and blessed tie
Binding kindred hearts together
As the years go passing by.

R Vincent

THE MATROSE

*(Written about St Mary's Church, Colchester,
the church runs adjacent to the Roman wall)*

To tell of one Royalist Gunner, a king's matrose,
who from St Mary's tower engaged his king's foes.
Climbing the church steps, cannon on his back,
he gained the necessary height to prevent an attack.

For days his skills kept the Roundheads at bay,
until inevitably the tower was shot away.
Known as Jack, but in rhyme this tale you know well,
for it's of his fall, and of Humpty Dumpty I tell.

Keith Leese

PRAISE FOR A SPORTING HERO

A legend in his lifetime
No need to give the name
His prowess reverberating
Through cricketing halls of fame
Not a man to take life quietly
No retiring violet he
A man who enjoys every moment
Of life with facility
A first class player
With all around ability
Giving watchers untold pleasure
With his outgoing personality
Not always appreciated
Sometimes hounded by the press
Always managed to rise above it
And cope with all the stress
Now retired from the field of battle
He regales us with clipped commentary
We still hear him tell it as it is
Long may this continue to be.

Barbara Williams

IT TAKES THE BISCUIT

Please give me a biscuit
With my cup of tea
Arrowroot or shortcake
It's all the same to me.

Chocolate, Digestive
Or even Lincoln creams
Malted milk or Ginger Snaps,
Or maybe some Peak Freans.

I like to dip them in my tea
Until they're soft and slushy
Sometimes they drop into the cup
Because they go too mushy.

When visitors come I ask them
Would they like a cup of tea
Then out comes the biscuit barrel
Full to the brim you see.

I keep an eye on what they have
In case they take too many
I put them away when they've had one or two
In case they don't leave me any.

Violetta Jean Ferguson

THE SHAWL

Life dawned 'midst Scottish Highlands,
With hills and heathers all around me.
Creation was by skilled, soft hands,
Amazing wonders I could see.
Gentle blending colours, curling bands
Like feathers swirling all around me.
Cool dainty fawns, like sun on sands
With shades of brown, for all to see.
Then came the day I'll not forget,
When voices spoke about my beauty.
Of my new owners I was told,
I also learned my future duties.
A sweet girl child I would enfold,
To keep her warm and safe from cold.
Since then a hundred years have passed,
And all my work is done at last.
You see I am a Paisley shawl,
And much admired by one and all.

Betty Smyth

WHY THE LIES

Why does everyone lie to me?
Have I got a sign across my face?
Is it because they can't keep the pace?

Some kind of need to lie to me,
I really can't figure it out.
What is this lying thing about?

Why can't anybody tell the truth?
Is it such an incapable thing,
Or is it because to them I bring,

The excuses they really need,
To continue with their lying,
Even if I lie here dying?

H E Oliver

INTERFERING

Pull yourself together for me,
Things can't be that black.
Tomorrow's another day my friend,
There's always some way back.
'How the hell would you know?
You've never been in my place,
Don't tell me how to live my life,
Stop shoving it in my face.'
But, things are what you make them,
I'm saying it for the best.
Cheer up, try to be happy.
Live life like the rest.
'You say it's for my own good
These things you're talking about,
But you don't understand my problems,
So, why don't you just - butt out?'

Rodney Epstein

NEARLY BUT NOT QUITE

I had a great opportunity of going gliding one day
This made me and my family quite excited I might say
The proceeds were for charity which made it worthwhile
So we all set off for the airport in Thame to fly in a different style
I might add, the weather had been brilliant the day before
and after the same
But on this particular day the forecast was not good
and looked like rain
We eventually found the airport that looked quite dead
A field, a pathway, plenty of grass and a dirty old shed
The field dipped over a hill, we could see nothing beyond
But drove up the field until our eyes did respond
There at the end stood these strange objects with wings
One with an open cockpit, no protection from the elements and things
Having made acquaintances, we added our names to the list
Somehow my name was the one they always missed
One large man sat in the front of the open type glider
I think the cockpit could have done with being a little bit wider
For, as the pilot fitted in by his side
I was wondering how this machine would take off and glide
My guess was not far wrong as they were launched into the air
They were not up for long as his weight did impair
He promised to give a pound to charity
For every minute he was up there
His donation was two pounds, I think the pilot was in despair
My son and granddaughter enjoyed their flight
When it came to my wife's turn black clouds were in sight
From then on the clouds opened and it poured with rain
My flight cancelled and have never been near a glider again.

Ralph Andrews

THE SYMPHONY OF LIFE

Everybody's a performer
In this stirring symphony
That carries on regardless
Of its changing melody,
But discord can necessitate
An even tempo to negate
The orchestra's uncertainty.

Not a player on this planet
Lacks the gift to orchestrate
The themes they have perfected
That their souls perpetuate,
And even harmonies that clash
Can alter lifetimes in a flash
With chordings that communicate.

When the players are performing
With innate dexterity
It's easy to distinguish
Life's incessant change of key,
And every movement justifies
The planned notation man applies
To forge a lasting harmony.

There are sounds that are uplifting
And a few that bring despair
To those who feel dejected
By their intermittent flair,
But life's composer will direct
And ultimately reconnect
The many notes in disrepair.

Everybody's a performer
In this vibrant symphony
That conjures up the music
Of a rare complexity,
And not an instrument refrains
From playing their melodic strains
That may last for eternity.

Iaian W Wade

WHEN I AM GROWN

When I am as big as Daddy, I wonder what I will be?
A fireman putting fires out or rescuing kittens stuck in a tree.
Maybe I'll be a policeman and catch robbers on the street
and wear a helmet on my head and have great big shiny feet.
Or should I be a doctor and give people pills to take,
or a bottle of nasty medicine when they get a tummy-ache.
What about a dentist? Looking at people's teeth,
and every time I pull one out, there's a new one underneath.
I really can't make up my mind, but I have loads of time
I don't need to work and pay the bills, as I am only nine.

Jane E Reynolds

BLESS THE CHILD

Bless the child who has nothing to eat.
Bless the child who has no shoes on her feet,
Bless the child with a heavenly smile
Please Lord, bless the child.

Protect the child without a home,
Protect the child with broken bones
Protect the child from all abuse
Please Lord, protect the child.

Love the child who's filled with despair
Love the child who needs someone to care.
Love the child who has been hurt deep inside
Please Lord, love the child.

K Arblaster

WHAT DO YOU WANT?

So what's your problem?
You have the vote
Elections are open
You chose who governs
Parliament must listen
So what's your problem?

You, who care and pray
You all worship the one God
Different buildings and chants
Different garb of religious gents
Different traditions, old history
Together we could care and pray.

Your problem in your home
Who rules there? Are they wise?
Do they want hatred to thrive?
Do they shout slogans?
Admire terrorists who died?
Want their children murdered?

Future with hope, happiness and joy
Is possible, if we can stop
The mantra of hatred.
Bred in ignorance and fear
The mothers should be teaching love
Demanding respect for life.

In religious wars, there are no heroes,
War is anger and contempt
Religion gives God's law, obey it
Blaspheme by twisting it for bigots
Let this generation have hope
Cry - brother, sister and love.

J Horsham

CAVERSWALL

From Cather's well to Caverswall, the time tracks call,
Where dark shadows of the past, across your land, fall,
In the lost centuries, shrouded by the mist of times long pall.
Back 6,000 years, we witness the hunters first foot fall.
And back yet further ran a mighty river, from a nearby glacial wall.
Its powers decreased to leave stagnant meres, and great boulders,
                              from an ice-flow crawl.
Now with new warmth, from tundra, to scattered woodland, grew an
                              oak forest tall.
The home of bear, boar and wolf, and the mightiest beast of all,
The wisent, the white ox, the belligerent bulls did bellow and call.
Time moves on, plants and animals arrived, then gone.
But the land like pages in a book, by stone and wood recall.
From a Saxon secondary settlement, grew a stone castle, a baronial hall.
Changes occurring slowly through the ages, yet its people scarcely
                              changing at all.
The old families remaining, villagers and farmers, rural labourers.
Born, worked, then their remains once more united with the land.
Be they, the humblest of peasants, or his Lordship grand,
So with wonder, hark to the myths, magic and the mystery of times
                              long haul.
From aeons and centuries past, this place to us still calls,
                    to enchant us all
From icy blast and forest vast, to man's conquest in the distant past.
This ancient place remains forever - *Caverswall.*

Jonathan Pegg

DAYS

Monday's child is rather fat,
Tuesday's child a spiteful cat,
Wednesday's child is big and selfish,
Thursday's child is fond of shellfish,
Friday's child will never sleep,
Saturday's child - a woolly sheep,
But the child that is born on the Sabbath day,
You'll find is mean and apt to stray.

V Chalmers

HOPE IN A CANDLE

Little candle, burning bright,
You understand my desperate plight,
I cannot see the way to go,
All my life seems full of woe.

I only have to look at you,
You seem to know the thing to do,
Peace and calm is all you know
You always know the way to go.

So why am I always worried?
Your way of life is never hurried,
I'll have to try and trust in you,
A better thing I couldn't do.

Sylvia McGregor

ON BECOMING AN OAP

        Hey!
I'm sixty
        Today
And I've just heard that my pension is to be four pence a week . . .

        Okay!
My hair may be
        Grey
And I may not now
        Play
Squash
Badminton
Or go rock climbing

But
I can walk on the beach on a blustery
        Day
Plan a journey to France for a weekend in
        May.

Paint, sing,
Write long letters to
My son
My MP and
My local paper

And listen to Andy (Williams)
   and Doris (Day)
On my old record player . . .
And eat chocolate.

   Hey!
It's good to be sixty
   Today!

Judy Rochester

PUDDING LANE

The homes are very old in Pudding Lane,
straw thatched, with walls of mellowed stone.
Cats sun themselves upon the tarmac path,
and wild flowers, at its edge, their seeds have sown.
What craftsmen built these ancient little homes,
whose massive beams support each cosy room,
and tiny windows peeping through the thatch,
reflect the light of early morn till noon?

Once a narrow road led to the Green,
and from whence a lane took folk to Oundle town,
or halfway, branched off up to Bareshank Wood,
whose boundaries were the ancient forest's crown.
What sights it must have seen, what tales to tell
of folk who lived here generations past.
The carpenter whose workshop graced the lane,
and whose ancient tools, did, for a lifetime last.

There are roses now around the cottage door,
and flowers beneath the ancient boundary wall,
and in the spacious gardens tucked behind,
are lawns, and fish ponds, and kitchen gardens small.
No grunting pigs peep over crumbling sty's,
or scratching hens wire penned on little plots.
No rabbits in their hutches lie in wait for
cabbage leaves, and carrots, unfit for cooking pots.

Sweet homes in Pudding Lane, what sights you've seen
from centuries past until the present day,
part of you is now no more, so doubly dear
are those still rising from their beds of rock and clay.
No masons live to build them like this now
from rule of thumb, and keen and practised eyes,
with roofs that warded off the rain and snow,
and squat stained chimneys pointing to the skies.

Mary Ward Hunt

OUR DYING DEEDS

our dying deeds, dreamless in the day,
of light and night, scorn the all-taloned ark.
our dying deeds, all-scheming in the grey.

christ dreams death, as the sun inside red may
in shimmering crown, lets light mete the dark.
our dying deeds, all dreamless in the day.

love cracks the skulls of the sun-fawning play
of the bright, delighting in death's green park.
our dying deeds, all-scheming in the grey.

christ strips the mind of its sea-spurning flay
as the blue hounds of life must gleam and spark.
our dying deeds, all dreamless in the day.
our dying deeds, all-scheming in the grey.

Jim Bellamy

Do You See The Things I See?

Do you see the things I see
Through your eyes of destiny?
Can I touch or hold your hand
Grab the light and make a stand?

Do I wonder where I go
To a place where my blood will flow?
Kiss the sea and live in denial
Walk on the lonely path of trial.

Do you see the things I see?
Take my hand come dance with me
Can I touch or hold your hand?
Feel the wind blow on the sand.

Do I wonder where you went?
You can't know how much that meant.
Taste my tears and kiss my lips
Watch me crumble into little bits.

Do you see the things I see
Through your eyes of destiny?
Do you see the things I see?
Take my hand come dance with me.

Neil Webber

FIND ME A WIFE, DAD

Dad, I don't want a girl who's sporting flat feet,
Or a laugh that will wake up the rest of the street.
I'd like her mature, but not over the hill
And not one that fidgets or mumbles at will.

Dad, I don't want her body to be big, round and fat,
I'm not all that choosy, but I don't fancy that.
A beautiful face with luscious sweet lips,
No bulging thighs, just well-rounded hips.

Dad, I don't want her hair to be lank or too short,
And please not a girl that plays lots of sport.
She's got to like animals, especially dogs,
But I'm not really bothered if she's frightened of frogs.

Dad, I don't want her eyes permanently looking at the sky,
'Cause I've always found that type are cunning and sly.
She doesn't need to be rich and have lots of cash,
And please, no one sickly and covered in a rash.

Dad, I don't want a woman whose brain has gone west,
I think above average, that would be best.
Now as for her feet, I think a size four,
But no painted nails, I don't want a whore.

Dad, I don't want my wife to have long facial hair,
I'm not that particular, but people would stare.
No rounding shoulders or a stoop or a hunch,
And no rickety joints that clatter and crunch.

Dad, I don't want a girl whose cooking is vile,
And when I tell jokes, she must at least smile.
Her hands must be dainty, not callused and rough,
And a sweet tender voice not uncivil and gruff.

Dad, I know it's a cheek to give you this quest,
But I'm sure you'll oblige and give it your best.
I could have asked Grandad or maybe my brother,
But Dad you're no fool, just look at my mother.

Garry Knowles

TRUE

Let you into a little secret
If you hold it, you will keep it.
Trust your soul to tell you what to do,
Ensure that you are true to you.
Whisper to yourself as your guide
Go with what you feel inside.
Don't regret and be what you will
Until you can rest and just be still.

Julie White

BLOOMERS IN THE BALLROOM

This attractive lady from near Halfway
Went to a dance there one day,
Her face wore a frown
When her skirt fell right down,
She didn't know what to say.

Her husband named Dave
Said, 'That sure was some rave
But you mustn't do that every day,
For the next time you do
I'll form up a big queue
And then get them all to pay!'

Fred Grimwade

NEW P'SU

There is a washing liquid
Called 'all new P'su'
It washes clothes so very well
It's true, it's true, *it's true!*

I washed my granny's bloomers
In 'all new P'su'
They started off red and white
And finished navy blue.

Andrew Younger

A STORM AT SEA

A dismal angry sea makes the ship sway,
As a wave creeps in the gap with a spray,
Tall black masts block out the moon,
The deck creaks and groans a tune,
Clouds rumble loud with thunder,
As I grip the wheel,
Will I last through it all I wonder,
My eyes are round with fright,
As I try to peer through the night,
My stomach's churning,
The wheel keeps turning,
The wind is my only guide,
As my strength cannot fight the tide.

Angela Johnson

SISTERS

One day last week I went to see,
One of my younger sisters called Marjorie,
We shared a meal, wine, and had a chat,
Then acted like wild feral cats.

Our clothes were neat, and we looked smart,
But we laughed and giggled like silly tarts,
We talked about men, to pass the time,
The things we said (must have been the wine).

In her bedroom, we tried on clothes,
In our 'frilly nillys', (with her curtains closed)
I am the elder of we six, and I must say
That I'm glad we sisters can still play.

Then she told me my young face was looking old,
But we both have more 'white hair' than gold,
Marjorie told me she was going to dye my hair,
Even if she had to 'strap me' to her chair.

My 'white hair' makes me look wise,
Shhh, (I still get winks off younger guys)
Marjorie's going to dye my hair to blonde,
I wish she'd just 'wave' a magic wand.

But she's always been 'bossier' than me,
Even though last weekend. I turned (shhh) fifty.

Susan Carole Roberts

ET

h time to gaze
id smoky haze,
d blackest night,
sful sight,
s in a daze
hen he sways,
eyes have a glaze,
his plight,

Try to forget, in vain erase,
A man disturbed, his mind a maze,
As life goes on with fervent might,
It's left a mark, however slight,
And thoughts return with silent praise,
Oh, life is sweet.

Wilhelmina Cobb

TURNER'S TEMERAIRE

O gallant Temeraire
Thru each war you bravely fought
Giving comfort to your men
With each battle that they sought
Sheltered them from harm
When they were ill or dying
Sailed waters that were calm
Whilst they regrouped for trying

But sadly at your end
These men forgot all this
As you sailed home in triumph
Masts tall in all the mist

But one man painted you
As he witnessed your demise
The artist Turner cold and blue
Made your portrait light the skies

Now you are remembered
Looking battle-worn
Forever sailing home
With face towards the dawn.

Fritzi Newlands-DuBarry

EXIT

I was too late, the clock had run out of hours,
Standing wistfully at your garden gate
Smelling the scent of your garden flowers
I regretted being too late.

Time has never been my friend
It has always used me cruelly
I never thought that time could end
The meaning you have had for me.

The windows stared like soulless eyes
Upon my final humiliation
Too late for love, too late for lies
I reached my deserved destination.

You had left this, your world's end
It must have been so hard for you
And I remember sadly that I didn't spend
One hour longer than I had to

It's too late now to understand my ways
And how much you really meant to me,
You were the linchpin of my golden days
I never meant to make you lonely

Carol Pidgeon

FLIGHT OR FANCY

Travel me to anticipate
Your life far and wide.
Happy I home to reside
Where next you decide.

My leisure labour comfort
Your suitcase to passport.
Seaside outing occasionally
Land, sea, air transport.

Home clothes so casual
Yours may be travel smart.
My best for occasions
Travelwear you're an art.

Yearly our various seasons
Each to his own way adjust.
Cold of winter scene
Warm home wear mine
Your travelwear no fuss.

Your warm flight destination
My winter months to face.
Happy are you your way
Happy am I in my place.

Victoria Joan Theedam

A DAY IN THE STORES

Working in a warehouse with colleagues and at times by yourself
Involves duties of unpacking, counting and locating the stock on a shelf.
You need to be numerically minded, knowing that one can count
By dealing with orders received and accepted to the precise amount.

Identification of stock whilst receiving goods is all part of the game
Due to lots of items within the stores that can easily look the same.
Receiving damaged and incorrect stock or an order of shortfall
Has to be recorded and reported to the supplier by a telephone call.

Annual stocktakes are required and can certainly take a while
Ensuring that a manual count agrees with a computer just to reconcile.
And having to be accurate when items are issued to the workshop floor
As they could return behind your back and help themselves to more.

The storeman could be in a position where he's simply out of luck
Having to unload deliveries manually, but is saved by the forklift truck
And setting delivery times is better than letting them just arrive
Especially when a day's stores work is complete at the closing time
- of five.

Paul Clifton

ALAN SIMMONS - THIS IS YOUR LIFE

Three rounds of *'Hoots Mon'* and
'Fight The Good Fight'
This was the answer I got on that night,
When I asked our Alan, my brother-to-be,
Which hymns for their wedding,
That's what he told me.

Always the joker, always the clown,
A man full of laughter, and not one to frown.
A tease to assistants in bookies and shops,
A man full of kindness, not one for the hops.
He liked to play bingo, for years, liked a fag,
But there really was little made him lose his rag.

He adored his grandchildren, son Gary and wife,
And he cherished Maureen, the love of his life.
His life was his family, his garden and all,
Though when he was young, he was good at football.
For Woodhouse West End, he played goalie at peak,
We used to support them, each Sat'day each week.

A spell in the Army, some time in Hong Kong,
Left him with malaria, on and off, all life long.
His motorbike, his pleasure when he returned home,
Then he met our Maureen, so no more to roam.
Many years in the pit left him weak in the chest,
A big strapping bloke, who was one of the best.
They had forty plus years of happy-wed life;
This wonderful man and our Maureen, his wife.

Now he has left this mortal coil,
To seek that long-earned rest,
But I bet the angels are giggling,
At our Alan, who is Heaven's new guest.

Eileen Moody Burton

PLEASE ALLOW

Let me weep gentle tears though I don't cry
Let the wind rage and clouds blacken the sky
Let man rampage the Earth, earthlings to die
Let them fight their own battles in their way
Let them know life's a visit, yesterday
Let man create in his own image, yea
Let light into darkness, we all can see
Let burdens get lighter for you and me
Let babies cry and stretch their lungs, set free
Let young life explore and not reason why
Let us all be courageous, can we try
Let me weep gentle tears though I don't cry.

Elizabeth Boultwood

No Contest

She should be up in high finance,
She always draws the lucky chance,
Park Lane she buys, wins beauty prize
While I pay super tax.

With card, from jail she gets out free
And buys another property
Proceeds past 'Go' - I told you so -
I get doctors' bills.

Mayfair hotels she can afford,
She practically owns the board,
I throw the dice - how very nice -
I get Old Kent Road.

My bankruptcy is well in sight,
I'm really in a sorry plight.
I try in vain to miss Park Lane,
Monopoly is not my game!

K B Law

TIME

Time is short when you're getting older
We must sit up and start to get bolder
So much we can do, no matter what age
There's nothing worse than being locked in a cage.

Some have talent, some can try
Never let time get the better, just fly.
As the saying goes 'tempus fugit'
Grab it now, you know you can do it.

Many say when years have gone by
I'd wish I'd done that and then cry.
Those who hesitate are always lost
When time has gone we pay the cost.

So make use of time while you have it
Letting time pass almost becomes a habit.
It's too precious to let fade away,
Wake up, wake up, and start today.

Penny Money

DONKEY DRIVEL

Why is it all do lay ridicule,
That I am such a fool?
Beast of burden! They call me.
Some truth to that I do see!
For *your* being here with me -
Is a burden that weighs heavy!

See this mark upon my back?
It's the 'blessing' that you lack!
Heaven waits for me. Yes, indeed.
Payment for my ancestor's deed.
The King of Kings on, *us*, was borne,
To the said stable to be born.

What did *your* ancestor do there?
Other than just bleat and stare!
What real importance do you hold,
That makes you dare be so bold,
As to believe yourself more in favour,
With Him. *My* sweet Saviour?

The name? Lamb! That's a laugh!
If you think that - you are daft!
So what if his name's the same?
Lamb of God! It's just a name!
When you grow up yours will be 'ewe',
Then *He* won't be named after *You!*

No. The name, Lamb, you can't keep.
You'll just be a . . . Sheep of Sheep!
I'm not lying. Just you wait and see -
Then you can apologise to me.
When all of time has come to pass -
It won't be, *me*, everyone calls an *ass!*

Donna June Clift

LAST WALTZ IN LOVE

Seeping through my mind like the oil inside a well
Thick and black and treacherous
A thought I cannot tell
If true it means the end of this
If false it means I'm mad
It means that I have lived a lie
Your love I never had.

Did you really take her to your bed
When we were barely wed
Did you tell her she was beautiful
But marry me instead?
Did you find in her the things I lack
Or did you play her false?
Have we been playing poker
Or is this our final waltz?

Judy Climer

THE ISLAND IN THE SKY

The sky is orange, in places,
and the clouds are tall, like mountains in the sky,
the blue bits of sky are like the sea.
This is our island in the sky,
made up of clouds as they drift by.
My mam turned her head to me and said,
'I'd love to live there, wouldn't you?'

Christopher Carl Steward (11)

EUROTOUR 2001

Starting from London to Paris by coach,
Avignon, Marseilles and Nice to approach,
A swim in the Med, then Venice to see,
St Mark's, Doge's Palace, Lido for free.

Switzerland, United Nations and Bern,
Geneva, Lausanne, Montreux and Lucerne,
Then south to visit the city of Rome,
Ferry to Corfu and Athens to roam.

The Bosphorus and mosques in Istanbul,
Orient Express Vienna to pull,
Budapest, Vienna, Prague and Berlin,
On to Oslo and fjords near Bergen.

Finally back to Amsterdam city,
And London after holiday pretty.

Susan Mary Robertson

SHIPWRECK

The air was clear, though the sky was grey
And the tide on the ebb, I remember,
Leaving the sand white foamed on its way,
That cold morning in December.

There were two of us only on the beach at play,
Making footprints in the sand,
Lost in the pleasure of childhood that day,
But old enough to understand.

The war was in its second year,
We knew there were folks we would see no more,
For safety's sake we were sheltered here,
No bombs fell on this western shore.

And then we noticed other things,
Along the silent beach,
Silent, that is, except for the waves,
That brought them within our reach.

A shoe, a shirt, a broken chair,
The sodden picture of a bride,
A lifebelt which revealed from where
These tragic relics came with the tide.

The pathos of a Santa Claus,
Departed from his cake,
And Yuletide decorations
Swept ashore in battle's wake.

The hopes and dreams, and seasons greetings,
From loved ones, now no more,
And the grief of cancelled meetings
Lie in awful sadness on our shore.

Denis Shiels

DOG EAT DOG WORLD

It's a dog eat dog world, old people scared to leave the house,
They walk down their familiar streets as quiet as a mouse,
Getting their act together, just to step outside,
Afraid of what their once friendly avenues have to hide,
Pensioners are murdered now, sometimes for a measly pound, how sad,
Others are beaten just for fun, I think the world's gone mad.

Any of these people that lost a loved one in the war,
Must wonder at times what their sacrifice was for,
They were told it would end tyranny, that the world would be a
                                                better place,
But when I look around there aren't many with a smiling face,
Their pension is a pittance, they struggle to make ends meet,
I feel so sorry for them as they walk along the street,
Yes, it's a dog eat dog world which I think is so sad,
Life was nicer yesterday, before the world went mad.

Maureen Arnold

NEED

I need a drink - help, what will I do?
I'm trapped in this chair, stuck and bound
My mouth is all dry, I can't feel my tongue
My legs all aquiver, my heart starts to pound.

I need a drink - help, what will I do?
My eyes gaze around and what do I see
I try to be calm and be part of the scene
I know I have time to jump up and be free.

I need a drink - help, what will I do?
The engines are revving, crew looks so calm
Lift-off is imminent,
Think not a mouse - *a man!*

I need a drink - help, what will I do?
It taxis the runway, I grab at my chair
I give out a sigh . . .
We're up in the air.

I don't need a drink
I've managed so far
But next time on holiday
I think I'll go by car!

Sandra Mason

NIGHTMARE

Why am I frightened of flying
To soar up into the skies?
They say there's no fear of dying
But I think they are telling me lies.

I read it in the paper
An engine fell off a plane
I'm sure I'll have a better chance
If the engine falls off a train.

The pilot speaks over the intercom
To welcome us aboard
He tells us not to fear the storm
That's in the weather report.

We'll soon be flying down to Spain
Where the weather is set fair
Now I'm shaking in my shoes
I'm sure we'll not get there.

The plane has left a drizzly scene
A bumpy flight ahead
I hear a loud explosion
Thank God, I've woken up in bed.

Pamela Baily

ESKIMOS' VESTS

I know that you think that I'm a pest,
But how often does an Eskimo change his vest?
What I'd really like to know,
Is how does he wash it with all that snow?
He hangs it on the line at his own cost,
Because it becomes quite stiff with frost.
Does he only wash his face?
He can't reach any other place!
It's enough to make a kitten purr,
Covered up with all that fur.
Has he got a great big zip,
To take off his clothes and go for a dip?
Is his flannel frozen too,
And the soap, and the loo?
Is the toilet paper soggy?
Is the toilet damp and boggy?
Does he slip and slice around
And finally end up on the ground?
I know that you think that I'm a pest,
But how often does an Eskimo change his vest?

Mary Crowhurst

BLIND DATE

I read your ad
and liked what it said.

Couldn't put a face
but wrote just in case.

It was a hilarious meeting
and will take some beating.

I was standing at one end
and you at the other end.

It was so funny
and the day was so sunny.

You turned your head as if to music
believe me it was so classic.

Your fringe in front looked cute
you definitely looked a beaut.

We recognised each other
to introduce we did not bother.

Now we are together
hope it is forever and ever.

Albert Moses

MR CANDYMAN

Candyman, Candyman
Give me a sweet
Sugar-free
And carob coated
I deserve a treat
I've been working so hard
Counting all my toes
Looking at my garden
Watching how it grows.

Dear Mr Candyman
I don't have ten pence
But I may just sell this poem
If it can make sense
If I even sell with me
Or we can buy a seed
And plant an apple tree.

Thanks Mr Candyman
It's a lovely colour
I think I may cut it in half
And share it with my brother
If my brother likes it
He may just buy my poem
We're poor but we do part exchange
That's how we keep going.

Ibidola Odukoya

TEAPOT

The teapot is a funny bird
It leaps from bough to bough
And if it wants to make a brew
It needs to find a jug
That needs to find a cow.

The teapot is a silly bird
To help it I am able,
For when I got up this morning
I found one sitting on my table.

There was a bowl with sugar in
A cup and saucer too
A spoon to mix the whole thing up
Oh, I wish he only knew.

Well, the teapot is a giddy bird
I hope he comes to rest
For my parlour's quite the perfect place
For him to make his nest

John Green

TEMPORARY BLIP

They're fighting in the streets, fighting in the bars,
killing each other in motor cars.
Urban warriors, black and white,
like rats from the woodwork out in the night.

Jennifer walks, makes a wrong turn,
spins when she hears the tyres burn.
Headlights flicker, then flash by like stars,
one after another go racing in cars.

She steps back in horror, nearly cut down.
Heartbeats go faster on this side of town.
His breath makes war with her perfume.
She's another statistic, lost in the gloom.

Boy racers go spinning, drowning her screams,
killing her hopes, ending her dreams.
This is a country with get up and go,
glittering adverts, all just for show.

Now there's the sirens, like big cats gone mad.
Is this a city or an apple gone bad?
The economy's good, new jobs are announced.
Well there's one for the mugger and rapist who pounced.

He took Jennifer, left her for dead,
virginity ripped out, no young lover's bed.
The economy's slowing, a temporary blip,
time to get moving, find a big ship.

Islands of tower blocks light up the sky,
life specks inside them live and die.
Here lifts smell of urine, show messages of hate,
a whole world away from cottage and gate.

Life must adapt or it's no more.
That's why someone's got nine locks on the door.
Some have got guns, sticks or knives.
Some are too stoned to fear for their lives.

The economy's growing, Blair says it's so.
Don't sail away, please don't go.
No, don't panic, there's hope for us all.
England's a place where you can walk tall.

England's a planet, a world on its own,
where people are judged by the style of their phone.
England once swung 'like a pendulum do'
But spin now it does, like a drunk in a stew.

Robert Cook

COMPULSION

If I wasn't hooked on poetry,
I wouldn't burn the dinner.
If I never wrote another line,
I'm sure I would be thinner.
But when I get that need to write
And the urge is deep within,
I forget the saucepan on the gas
And it ends up in the bin.
It's then I eat the chocolate,
The fudge and other candy,
Nearby I keep the biscuit tin,
I need to know it's handy.
But if I gave up poetry,
Life wouldn't be the same
And when I felt like bingeing,
I'd have nothing left to blame.
I suppose I ought to try it
Before I get much fatter,
But I love my poetry and sweets,
So does it really matter?

June Marshall

HE'S HERE, HE'S THERE, HE'S EVERYWHERE

He's all over the globe, Tony Blair
One minute he's here, then he's there
Wherever there's strife
You'll find him with his wife
Saving the world from despair

One phone call from President Bush
Their bags are all packed with a rush
Then they take to the air
On a jet, in a blur
With much Labour spin and much fuss

Mistakes have been made, it's been said
There's one they'll recall with much dread
When Cherie forgot
To pack that red dot
She often slaps on her forehead

Now Tony Blair you'll agree
Has got that same look as JC
Yes there's something quite holy
And God-like with Tony
He sure puts the wind right up me

It's no secret our country of late
In everything is third rate
So please President Bush
Send someone to us
For we're in a hell of a state

Doug Sharkey

LIFE

Life's too short to quarrel
So make it up today,
It only brings you sorrow
As you go upon life's way.
Bring things out in the open
And discuss the reason why
You are not caring, or tomorrow
You may sigh.
For a friendship that was happy,
Then in anger it was lost,
It had stood the test of time,
Now you've lost it to your cost.
Life can be so fleeting, when the golden
Hours fly, and all your happy meetings
End up by severing ties.
Take every opportunity, to keep your
Quarrels in check, you will survive
Another day, of friendship, as you would
Expect, look out for Giant Discontent, and
Old Giant Despair, they're always waiting
In the wings, to trap you unawares.
If you have your health and strength
Say thank God for that, come back all that
You had said, and say amen to that.

Rosemary Peach

GENTLY, GENTLY

The old clock's pendulum gently swings,
Flickering firelight its brass face shows,
While on the hob a big black kettle hums and sings
As the old lady rocks slowly to and fro,
Her gnarled hands resting on her knee,
Sewing dropped, forgotten as she drifts to sleep.

Gently, gently fall the shadows now set free,
As the mild autumn breeze pauses to peep
In the window, past the fading flowers,
Stirring the curtains with an unseen hand,
And still she sleeps through the evening hours,
Till the fire glows low as she steps into another land.

Julia Frost

A NEW BEGINNING

Here we are, back together again
No more hurt, no more pain
Promises, statements, have been made
Rules and regulations to be laid

No more, are you out every night
Just a few evenings, is proper and right
There are so many things that we can do
With our boys, or just us two

We have already started to talk and plan
For a better future, if we can
A far way, there is to go
The road is long, and will be slow

All those nights I sat alone
Just waiting by the telephone
Sometimes till late at night
At the end of the tunnel, is there a light?

I used to try so hard with you
Hoping one day, you would try too
Often giving a card or gift
To show my love or give you a lift

I know you're sorry, you've proved it to me
You tell me at last, you don't want to be free
When you come home, you kiss and hug
My heart strings, you, at last do tug

Weekends are now looked forward to
To walk, talk, and laugh with you
Movies, meals or just stay in
We even cemented it with a new ring

Our future together is now to remain
Apart, we will never be again
Sometimes, I remember and I cry
But I know I love you,

Don't I?

Julie Livett

THE TEDDY BEAR

'Oh Mummy,' said a little girl,
'Could I have a teddy bear like other girls and boys?'
But Mummy replied with a heavy sigh,
One tear fell and she began to cry.
'I'm afraid your daddy's out of work with no pennies to spare,
So forget the teddy bear.'
Well, crafty Mary thought, 'I'll help my mother in the house,
In secret, when she has her daily nap.
I'll tidy my room and sweep the floors,
To try to help her with her chores,
While she's out of the way behind closed doors.'
At the end of the week at supper time,
A note was placed on mother's plate.
'Whilst you were asleep, I swept and dusted,
I've earned the money for my teddy bear.
How much money have you to spare?'
'Mary, I admire the work you've done,
If Daddy cannot spare the cash, nor can I,
Forget the teddy bear, that's trash.
I love you Mary, do you love me?
That is the question, please answer me
In dealing with this question honestly.'

Yvonne Rossiter

A CHANCE MEETING

A young man was walking alone one day,
When he met a young lady going that way.
He spoke to her, for she looked rather sad,
But she said to him, 'Oh, I'm not too bad.'

And then for a while they talked to each other,
And the lady made known she had not a good mother.
That her life at home was not too good,
For she was not being treated in the way that she should.

The man did not wish to interfere,
But wanted to help her as she seemed so sincere.
So he invited her to go for a walk,
And together they went and had a good talk.

She told the man about her life,
And how she longed to be someone's wife.
And said to him, 'What can I do?
For I'd love to have a man like you.'

He said to her, 'Well, I don't mind,
You seem to be one of my kind.
If it is your wish, I will fall in line,
And from today you shall be mine.'

'So let's get on and say no more,
Although we've never met before.
Our meeting now is forever and ever,
And we shall share our happiness together.'

W Woodward

ANCHOR BOOKS
SUBMISSIONS INVITED
SOMETHING FOR EVERYONE

ANCHOR BOOKS GEN - Any subject,
light-hearted clean fun, nothing unprintable
please.

THE OPPOSITE SEX - Have your say on the
opposite gender. Do they drive you mad or can
we co-exist in harmony?

THE NATURAL WORLD - Are we destroying
the world around us? What should we do to
preserve the beauty and the future of our planet -
you decide!

All poems no longer than 30 lines.
Always welcome! No fee!
Plus cash prizes to be won!

Mark your envelope (eg *The Natural World)*
And send to:
Anchor Books
Remus House, Coltsfoot Drive
Peterborough, PE2 9JX

**OVER £10,000 IN POETRY PRIZES
TO BE WON!**

Send an SAE for details on our New Year 2002
competition!